GONNA
BAKE ME A
RAINBOW
POEM

GONNA BAKE ME A RAINBOW POEM

A Student Guide to Writing Poetry

by Peter Sears

With poems by student winners of
the Scholastic Writing Awards

SCHOLASTIC INC.
New York Toronto London Auckland Sydney

ISBN 0-590-43085-8

12 11 10 9 8 7 6 5 4 3   0 1 2 3 4 5/9

Printed in the U.S.A.   40

First Scholastic printing, September 1990

Acknowledgments

I want to thank the young writers whose poems are in this book and all the young writers who submitted work to the Scholastic Writing Awards Program. I want to thank their English teachers and their parents for encouraging this self-expression. Lastly, I want to thank Editor Greg Holch for his superb work of fashioning the huge manuscript I gave him into a clear, focused book.

To my grandparents, Arthur and Antoinette Lockett

Contents

Introduction 1

1 "I" Poems 3

2 "You" Poems 12

3 Choosing a Subject 18

4 Language and Punctuation 27

5 Imagery, Simile, Metaphor 38

6 Associations 45

7 Irony and Satire 52

8 Fantasy 59

9 Lyric Poems 69

10 Rhyme 73

11 Love Poems 81

12 Growing Old 87

13 Making a Statement 94

14 Poetry and Art 100

15 A Word About Writing 108

16 Creative Thinking 114

Index of Poems   133
Index of Poets   137
About the Scholastic Awards Program   141
About the Author   143

GONNA
BAKE ME A
RAINBOW
POEM

Gonna Bake Me a Rainbow Poem

We stirred up
some red and orange
and blue and purple
in our momma's pan —
Melted a lotta'
Jimbo's crayons

Then they stuck
to the bottom
Me and my friend
SCRAPED AND SCRAPED
with a butter knife
until . . .
My momma walked
through the door

Lotsa' yellin'
Lotsa' cryin'
My friend left

All I wanted
was a rainbow —
Don't like this
gloomy weather

AMY WILSON

Introduction

Is Amy Wilson a famous poet? No. Amy Wilson wrote "Gonna Bake Me a Rainbow Poem" in 1981 as a senior at Ardmore High School in Ardmore, Oklahoma. She is an admirer of the painter Georgia O'Keeffe, and writes her poems while listening to music. Amy wrote, "Poetry is a good way to express thoughts. I average 20 drafts per poem." I hope Amy is still writing poetry.

*   *   *

My name is Peter Sears. I like to write, teach, play sports, be a good husband, and a good dad. I will be your guide through this book. You may not need one — the student poems speak for themselves. I hope you enjoy the poems. I do. In fact, the idea for this book came from my admiration of student writing. Some years ago I served as a preliminary judge for the Scholastic Writing Awards Program in the poetry division. Many of the poems I read were wonderful. I thought: Wouldn't it be great if students all over the country could see these poems? And a second thought: Wouldn't these poems make for an interesting book about writing poetry for students? I suggested the idea to Scholastic. Its president, Mr. Richard Robinson, encouraged me to make the book. Scholastic provided me with the winning poems from the years of the Writing Awards Program since the last Scholastic student poetry anthology. I set

1

to work, reading all the poems. I was overcome by how many fine poems I had. Choosing was difficult. I also had the poets' descriptions of how they came to write the poems. These comments were submitted on information sheets along with their poems. They included many suggestions for writing poems. I have incorporated many of their comments into this book.

I wish there had been a book like this when I was growing up. I might have liked poetry then. The poems I read in school did not include any by students. The poems did not interest me much. Not until college did I become interested in poetry. When I became an English teacher and a writer, I always wanted to do a poetry book for students by students. Every single poem in this book was written by a student. These poems show you that you can write a poem, too — that you can write about anything you want and in any way you want. Poetry writing provides you the opportunity to express yourself. You might like that. I hope you like the book. I sure liked making it.

PETER SEARS
PORTLAND, OREGON

1

"I" Poems

What is the best subject for a poem?

No, let me ask that another way.

Who is the best subject for a poem? For any kind of writing, for that matter. Well? Come on, say it.

"I am!"

When writers offer advice about how to become a writer, one of the points you will often hear is that you should write about what you know best. You are the best subject for your writing, and you can prove it. Just ask yourself, whom do you know the most about?

Whose feelings do you know most deeply?

Whose ideas do you know the best?

"Mine," right?

What does this mean? It means that you are a wonderful subject for your writing. It means that you have an infinite source for writing because you are always having experiences, and getting ideas.

Let's see an example. Well, you could just say things about yourself, like this:

Cheddar Cheese and Chocolate Cake

I am crazy about rich, dark, espresso coffee.
I am addicted to extra-sharp cheddar cheese and
　chocolate cake.
I never tire of window-shopping or munching crisp
　apple pies from Burger King.
I can consume a whole package of Wheat Thins while
　curled up reading a favorite novel.
I wear purple eyeshadow and pink nail varnish —
　always.
I love to laugh and scream for joy, to sing at the top of
　my voice.
I like to play heavy rock loud enough to burst your
　eardrums.
I like crazy parties, whipped cream, and solitude.

JULIET GAINSBOROUGH

Fun? Silly? Easy? Dumb? Honest? Real?

Whatever you think, try writing one yourself, just for fun.
Try starting each line with "I," and make one statement after
another.

About what? About anything!

I like the fact that the first four of the eight statements of
this poem are about food. Do you have a special dish that is
your favorite but that no one else likes? If you do, you could
start your poem with it, or end with it.

I'll tell you what else I like about this poem. I like the last
word of the fifth line, "always." The word gives a little extra
kick to the line. And I like the last line especially. The last
word, "solitude," is great at the end. It surprised me. I like the
combination "solitude" makes with the two other things, "crazy
parties" and "whipped cream." An interesting trio.

4

Juliet Gainsborough wrote this poem in 1982 when she was in the eighth grade in Placerita Junior High School in Valencia, California. Juliet says, "When I decide to write a poem, I usually write it straight down without an outline, but then I go back and write about five more drafts before I finish."

A "draft" is a version. Writing five drafts is a lot of work. But if you like the poem you are working on, writing another draft (writing it over again) can be fun. What's important, though, is getting the phrasing just the way you want it. You might get the poem right in one shot, if you're lucky. Read it over again. You may find something that you would like to change or add to. The smallest detail can lead you back into the creative burst that you started with; and touching back into this energy, this excitement, can lead in all sorts of directions. You may find your poem developing in ways that surprise you and that you like. Poetry is easier to tinker with and revise than, say, fiction is.

Noah de Lissovoy wrote the next poem in 1983 as a freshman at Evanston Township High School in Evanston, Illinois. Noah, who played in the jazz band, said his writing has been influenced by such writers as Ivan Turgenev and Willa Cather. "Walking in December," he said, is "about the joy of living" and was inspired by the poetry of Walt Whitman.

Walking in December

My eyes, (which are certainly bluer now than
    usual),
cut with clean acuity to clear light and the
    skeletons
of trees.

My dormant ears are pinched awake, to receive the
    conversations
of the birds and helicopters, zinging through the
    ether.

My stretching skin is slapped and stung.

My limbs, (which for once I recognize as limbs —
    and mine)
are ecstatic in their steady locomotion, and I
    become aware of the
hot blood coursing, blood pulsing through my
    veins.

A human steam engine, I churn down the
    sidewalk, unstoppable in
the pride of my mortality.

NOAH DE LISSOVOY

Discovery

Ah.
Here it comes again.
Giggling,
Effervescent,
It begins in the lowest levels of my belly,
Creeps up to engulf my heart,
Lightens my head.
It makes me dizzy.

Laughter bubbles about inside my mouth
Tickling my teeth
Dancing on my tongue . . .
Bursting out!
See how it brightens the sun,
Clears the skies,
Softens the rain.
Everyone smiles.
"She's in love," they whisper,
And I hear.
Am I?
I am . . . oh, yes,
I
Am.
I love the person
Who is
Me.

TONI MOSLEY

The ending of Toni Mosley's poem "Discovery" is a surprise. As a senior at William P. Boone High School in Orlando, Florida, Toni wrote "Discovery" in 1981. Toni said, "The inspiration comes from a moment or a day when a feeling is too strong for me to handle inside myself." An interesting way to look at poetry, don't you think? It certainly provides a strong reason to write — or to create in any art form!

7

I Am First-Person Singular

but wish I were third-person plural
and could watch you front and back
and could say
no, they did it.
I am wearing myself as a dress
    mother's earrings
    sister's Chanel
    father's mind
        opinions, grudges.
Oh, to be third-person plural
    never have to agree
    and be ambiguous with a cause
    decide by plurality.
Be angry, and say I was unjust
    and have reason yet for doing whatever I had done
    and be strong in numbers
and right in singularity
and love several people
    and never hurt one
and send one of me home
    if I got tedious
    or hopelessly immature
and no one would care
    they'd say, "Oh, she's a they."

KIMBERLY ROLLER

This poem has lots of surprises. That is what keeps it interesting. A line I really like is "I am wearing myself as a dress." Kimberly Roller wrote this poem in 1981 as a senior at Phillips Exeter Academy in Exeter, New Hampshire.

The Last Saturday

I remember sunny nights
when I threw yellow Frisbees
under plum trees and watched
the dusk turn into dark.

Threw rocks at the streetlights
and pinecones at passing cars
from behind the rows of overgrown
yew bushes staggering Buchanan St.

The Birdville tennis courts bounced
hockey pucks and the fence
grated the baseball fields
where crowds mimicked maniacs.

I left when I got tired
and sat on the back porch
cussing the mosquitos
and wishing I was older.

KEN KOSTKA

Ken Kostka is from Natrona Heights, Pennsylvania. He
wrote "The Last Saturday" in 1981 when he was a senior at
Highlands Senior High School.

In the poem "The Last Saturday," Ken is thinking back-
wards, not forwards. He is recalling evenings when he fooled
around along Buchanan Street. If you want to try writing your
own recollection, just start off "I remember," and then go into
any memory you think of. You can write your recollection as
prose (your usual way of writing) or as poetry. Pick anything

9

you want to write about. Try to keep it to one page to begin with.

Now that you have written one recollection, your mind is probably moving back in your memory to other experiences. You probably could write another recollection right now, and write it more easily than the first one. Here is another way to do it. Write three parts. Begin the first part with "In the mornings." Begin the second part with "In the afternoons." Begin the third part with "In the evenings." Where did I get this idea? Oh, it just came to me from out of the blue. No, it didn't. I got the idea from the next poem.

Summer in Kansas

In the mornings we run in packs
chased by jackrabbits and prairie chickens
through rows of wild wheat
over slowly rolling hills.

In the afternoons we paddle
through the only creek for miles,
later rest under cottonwoods,
watch the dust settle around us.

In the evenings we roam the plain,
seek the smell of familiar ground
where we will stretch our bodies
over dirt, listen to land
break like bones beneath us.

CHRISTINE MURRAY

10

Christine Murray wrote "Summer in Kansas" in 1982 when she was a senior at Interlochen Arts Academy in Interlochen, Michigan. The source of this poem wasn't inspiration. Christine says, "As for the other poems in my entry (including 'Summer in Kansas'), all were written in response to assignments."

Writing about yourself is a good way to get a poem going. You can have some fun, even in a serious poem. You can use true material, or you can make up everything. You can pretend you are someone else and write from that person's point of view.

Poetry is just one medium (means) for self-expression. Do you have a favorite? Music? Dance? Painting? Writing? There are many art forms. You might think about trying them all to find the one you like best. And you don't have to limit yourself to one.

2

"You" Poems

What do you think is the most personal kind of writing? Is it a diary? A journal? Is it a letter? Do you think that poetry is a personal form of writing? Poetry can, I think, convey a feeling of intimacy. One way to encourage this feeling is to write the poem *to* someone. The poet is the speaker, the "I," and the person being addressed is the "you." I like to call poems set up in this way "you" poems.

Sunwashed Windows

As I look out the window
and sunlight falls delicately upon my face,
embracing me with its warmth,
I think about you,
and everything that's happened between us
in such a short period of time,
and wonder, are you looking out the window
thinking of me?

HILWATHA STEPHENS

Hilwatha Stephens wrote this poem in 1982, while in the ninth grade at Marietta High School in Marietta, Georgia. This poem could be sent as a letter, couldn't it? It is personal and tender.

The Surface

You are
but a poor reflection
Of yourself.
You fool others
But you don't fool
me,
with your
cool, clear
unrippling
outer surface.
Others gaze at
you
And see themselves
in your careful
yet indifferent
reply
But I know
that behind
that cold perfection
Your blood runs
with mercury fire.
I have touched you
and come away
bleeding
from your razor
sharp edges —
that catch the poor
unwary people
who worship
you.

Dare I touch
again?

ELAINE NORMAN

Elaine Norman shows us with her poem "The Surface" how a "you" poem can be used to make an important distinction between what is and what seems to be. As critical as the poem is of the person it addresses, Elaine ends it with a question for herself, not the "you."

Elaine Norman wrote this poem in 1981 during her senior year at Mainland Senior High School in Daytona Beach, Florida.

On Sunday You'll Be Home

At Priest River you're probably
zipped into your boy scout sleeping bag,
listening to it rain on the cabin roof.
Tomorrow you'll get up, put on hip boots,
an orange stocking cap
that fits over your ears,
and row the boat
to the middle of Priest Lake.
You'll drop your line over the edge
and hope for good or better weather
by afternoon.
For dinner you'll eat fish,
picking the bones with greasy fingers,
or spitting them back
onto your plate.

14

You won't shower or brush your hair
and your socks will steam
when you prop your feet
close to the fire.
Your clothes and beard damp,
you'll fall into bed.
Before you sleep
you'll think of me.

JENNY CONNELLY

I believe it. I believe that the "you" of this poem will think about the speaker, the "me." The poem convinces me that the poet knows what she is talking about. I love the way I am brought into the life of the "you." I love the way the "you" is both talked to and talked about.

And what a great last line! It's a complete surprise. Yet once it's said, all the rest of the poem gathers together to back it up. The last line *is* the poem, in a way. I especially like its directness. "You'll think of me" is so much better than "maybe you'll think of me" or "I hope you'll think of me" or "you'll probably think of me."

Try a poem like this. Try starting off with the words "you're probably" somewhere in the first line, as Jenny Connelly does in "On Sunday You'll Be Home." Think of someone you like, and think of what he or she might be doing at a particular moment. Then just write a description of what the "you" is doing.

Write it in prose if you want to. Or write it first in prose, then change it into a poem. Just make line breaks where you want to. Make marks in the prose where you want to make line breaks, and copy it over following the line breaks.

Jenny Connelly works like this from prose to poetry. She writes in her comments, "When I begin a poem, I usually write

15

in prose form first, decide what I want the poem to say, then put it in line form. I read it aloud, make changes, and after about five drafts I begin concentrating on the individual words, punctuation, and line breaks." About writing "On Sunday You'll Be Home," Jenny says, "[It] came about while a close friend was on a weekend fishing trip. This poem was re-written quite a few times, and is nothing like the original draft."

Jenny Connelly wrote this poem in 1981 when she was a senior at West Valley High School in Spokane, Washington.

The Bird

You found the seagull on the beach
where it had died in its own red splash.
You picked the body up,
dug your thumb deep between feathers
and then let it drop like rock to the sand.

The stone that you had thrown
was sharp and glazed red.
You put it in your pocket
to keep as one of your treasures.

But now as you walk home
you force that stone into the grooves of your palm.
You imagine some bird's beak tear deep inside you,
and you are sure you feel something
fly from yourself into the clouds.

CURTIS RIDEOUT

16

Curtis Rideout was a junior at the Interlochen Arts Academy in Interlochen, Michigan, when he wrote "The Bird" in 1983. Curtis said that he liked the poets Ezra Pound, T.S. Eliot, Jim Harrison, and Richard Hugo because "they present emotions in a clean, sharp way, and they make a point through careful use of music and selection of words."

Curtis Rideout follows the examples of his favorite poets well. The poem makes us think about its subject. The ending is creepy and wonderful, and I can't help but think that the "you" of the poem is actually "I," the poet. I believe that Curtis Rideout uses "you" to make the poem even more powerful.

What do you think of "you poems"? Do you think they offer you more of an opportunity to write both personally and powerfully? Write a "you" poem of your own. You might begin by just writing down in prose everything you can think of, and then select the words or phrases that interest you, and try to shape them into a poem.

Choosing a Subject

Laughter

Pink bubblegum
Skips
Into my mouth.
Rippled mirth
Ricochets
From my teeth
And bubbling gaily
Over my tongue,
A stifled giggle
Struggles
To open my lips
With tickling fingers,
Swiftly dancing forth
In a bouncing crescendo
As it
Escapes.

PAMELA COBB

You don't need a serious subject for a poem. You don't need a fancy idea. You just need a place to start, a word, a phrase, or a scene. We've looked at poems about "I" and "you." But once you start thinking, poems have a way of gathering around any subject, even bubble gum.

Pick a common thing like bubble gum and try writing a poem about it. You might pick a fast food like french fries, or a hamburger, or a soft drink, or candy. Write about how much fun it is to eat or drink. Describe this exactly. Write any way you want in order to express how tasty it is, or how obsessed you are with it. You could be thinking about how wonderful it would be just to have that special something right now. Or you could write about how certain foods go with certain places, like popcorn with movies. Or you could write about pretending not to like something and sneaking it while no one is looking. These suggestions are just different ways to write a poem about some kind of food. You do it any way you like. Experiment. Try different ways if you want to.

Pamela Cobb wrote "Laughter" in 1981 as a ninth-grader at Pearl River High School in Pearl River, Louisiana.

Her poem "Laughter" is very imaginative. You can see this in the third word, "skips." What a good descriptive verb! As a matter of fact, all the verbs in this poem are interesting. The words are chosen carefully for this poem. They allow us, the readers, to feel what the poet is describing. This is a good poem, and fun to read. I'm sure it was fun to write.

Another good subject for a poem is a place. Think of a place, or setting, because a place has things in it that you can describe. Besides, if the setting is familiar to you, then you'll have memories of events that happened there. The setting can be anywhere you choose. It is natural to pick a place you like. Yet the setting needn't be nice. You can generate a poem out of any kind of setting, even one you don't like, perhaps because you want to express something about the setting.

19

Scene

Close by the door
of the
weathered old
shack plays a
child in a
flour sack
dress, her
cornhusk
ballerina
pirouetting
on a tinpail
stage.

MARY BETH CARVILLE

This poem is, as the title says, just a "scene." The poem is very exact. There are no extra words. The word "tinpail" hits with real impact. The word goes along with "shack," "flour sack," and "cornhusk" to create the real world of the poem, just as "ballerina," "pirouetting," and "stage" create the child's imaginary world. In a few words, the poet has expressed a lot.

Cloudy Fall Days

Cloudy fall days,
lying on your back in the brown grass
snuggling into the grayness
of an old sweatshirt.

Feeling the odds 'n' ends in your pockets
        a smooth horsechestnut,
the roughness of a sparkly rock,
a whispery thin strip of birch bark,
gritty crumbs of dirt,
the coldness of a jackknife.
Just lying there
letting your mind drift —
like the clouds
while they take the shape of your imaginings,
as a cold wind
with a promise of winter on its breath
stirs the leaves to life
dancing an ancient dance
in the cold gray emptiness
of the sky at sunset.

AMY ALBERT

Poet Amy Albert also writes about a place. She finds plenty
of good details about "just lying there." She isn't doing much,
and little is going on. Yet she conveys well how pleasant it is
just to be there. What a simple subject for a poem!

Amy Albert was a sophomore in 1982 at Rolling Meadows
High School in Rolling Meadows, Illinois, when she wrote her
poem "Cloudy Fall Days."

Night Slavery

Homework
Lay around me
Cluttered in
Mess of pens

And pencils.
The radio
plays softly to the accompaniment
Of water gushing,
Dogs barking.
I am lulled to sleep,
So tired, yet worried about
Insomnia and getting to bed late.
Homework,
Slave driver,
Relentlessly pushing me to anxiety.
Hunched over my desk
My world for the moment,
A universe of
Papers, folders, and assignments.
The room around me reverberates
To the sounds of
My father snoring and
Cars going by
Like nightmares
Disturbing
The peace of sleep.
The rain
A roll of drums
Pounding upon my brain
Slamming in the fear of oversleeping
Like a hot poker.

People talk
The fan whirrs.
I cannot think!!
Sound is my enemy,

Cutting off the brain's
   ability to think.
But suddenly,
Like a quieting maternal hand upon
A frantic infant,
The gecko and papaya bird
In sweet harmony
Restore order and
Tranquil repose upon the
Hysteria of my
   Mind.

CHRISTINE MCLEAN

Christine McLean wrote her poem "Night Slavery" in 1983 as an eighth-grader at the Kamehameha Schools in Honolulu, Hawaii.

Sometimes a poem can appear to be about one subject while actually being about something else. This makes for a tricky poem. It can appear simple while actually being pretty complex.

Let the Geese Fly

South they go
And the north wind
Pushes
Giving them a hand.

The sound of the wind
Calls them on
Strengthening their journey.

Are they sure?
Will my Grandma be okay
When they come back again?

ELIA LANDE

Elia Lande wrote this poem in 1982 as a seventh-grader at the Masterson School in Philadelphia, Pennsylvania.

"Let the Geese Fly" is a short poem, which contains no difficult words. So it should be pretty simple. Well, is it? What do you think?

There are two questions you can ask about any poem. First, what is the subject of the poem? Second, what is the poet's attitude toward the subject of the poem?

The subject of this poem is the migration of geese. All right, then what is the poet's attitude toward the subject? He says that the geese are flying south, and he describes how the north wind assists them in their flight. Then he asks a question about the geese: "Are they sure?" Sure of what? And then he asks a question about his grandma. What does his grandma have to do with the geese?

This poem may be confusing. After eight lines about the geese the poet finishes the poem with two lines about his grandmother. This poem is harder than many of the poems we have read, even though it may look simple.

If the poem is confusing, let me try to make sense out of it. The first two sections, or stanzas, of the poem do not present a problem. The problem arises in the last stanza. Perhaps the crucial line is "Are they sure?" The poet is asking if the geese are sure about their flying south. Somehow this question leads to the next question. How these two questions relate may be the key to the poem. Does this sequence of questions in the last stanza make sense to you?

It seems that the poet may be worried about his grandmother. Perhaps she is sick or very old. He is worried that she is not going to live much longer. But what does the way the poet feels about his grandmother have to do with geese flying south? Think about this question. It may spring the poem open for you.

Geese fly south in the winter and return north in the spring. This is their migrational pattern. They do this year in and year out. What, then, is the answer to the poet's question about the geese? He asked about the geese, "Are they sure?" Of course, they are sure. Their migration is instinctive. The poet knows the geese will be back. I think he is asking the question to get his courage up to ask the real question: "Will my Grandma be okay/ When they come back again?" The poet wants to be sure that his grandma will live at least a while longer. Since there is no way to be sure of this, he makes up a way to try to convince himself. This is natural. Trying to face up to the eventual death of someone you love is very difficult. In fact, just raising the question is hard.

You might ask, then, if the poem is an expression of the poet's hope that his grandmother will live a little longer, why all the talk about geese? Why is most of the poem about the geese and only a small part of it about his grandmother? I bet you can answer this question. Describing the migration of the geese allows the poet to raise the question of his grandmother in a way that will let him believe that she will not die soon. So the poem really is about the geese. They are very important to the poet. And the poem is also about his grandmother. More specifically, it is about his hope that his grandmother will not die soon. What, then, is the poet's attitude toward his subject? He hopes that just as the geese will fly north again, his grandmother will go on living, at least until they return.

What I have written here is an interpretation of the poem "Let the Geese Fly." It is an interpretation because we don't know what the poet has in mind. There are other possible interpretations. The best interpretation offers a sensible reason for every question a reader can raise about a poem.

"Let the Geese Fly" demonstrates that some subjects are emotionally too difficult to address directly, right at the start of a poem. The poem demonstrates, too, that what appears to be a simple poem about a clear subject can change, right under your eyes, into a more complex poem.

What I admire about this poem is that once it reaches its real subject, it doesn't spend a lot of time explaining. Instead, it addresses its subject directly: it poses the central question. That takes some courage because the reader can become confused.

You might try writing a poem like "Let the Geese Fly." Here is how you do it. You start describing something. Then you move quickly to something personally important to you, that you think of before or while writing your description. You might enjoy this way of writing a poem.

Language and Punctuation

Poetry is made up of words, so the kinds of words — the language — a poet uses characterize that poet's work. But what does it mean to speak of different kinds of words, or different kinds of language?

Request to a Minstrel

Sing unto me a song of seasons
    Of death, rebirth and happiness.
Sing unto me a song of reasons
    Staid thoughts, and deepest contemplations.
Sing unto me a song of sorrows
    Quiet longing and dark despair.
Then, sing to me a song of tomorrows
    Of joy and laughter:
        tarry longest there.

ANDREA COX

How would you describe the kind of words in "Request to a Minstrel"? Would you call them old-fashioned? Traditional? Formal? Each of these adjectives would do just fine.

Perhaps you like this kind of language. Perhaps you don't. But an important question is whether or not this kind of language seems to be appropriate to what the poet is expressing. It seems to me that the kind of language of this poem is appropriate to minstrels, to poetry of "olden days," wouldn't you say? If so, the purpose of the poem and the kind of language are well matched. This matching can also be called the matching of sound and sense, of music and meaning, of language and idea.

Seashore Girl

Hey
girl
hipswaying swirl
of colored cloth
Trot me down
a
song
singingsoftly curls
so
long
Icecreamcolored cheeks
gonna melt
into a
melody
for
me

That searolling stride
gonna sing me off
to
sleep

JAMES FARRER

The kind of language in this poem is certainly different from the kind of language used in "Request to a Minstrel." That doesn't mean, though, that the language of this poem isn't appropriate to its purpose. Do you think that the language of "Seashore Girl" fits the idea of the poem well?

Sometimes, the whole point of a poem, the spirit of the poem, is embodied in the language. For some poems there is no real difference between the kind of language used and the whole idea of the poem. I think this is true of "Seashore Girl," and I think it is true of other poems, but not all poems.

Here are some other poems in which the language is important.

You Haven't Got a Prayer

By God,
(diddy doo-wop)
I'm gonna getcha.
(diddy doo-wop)
I'm gonna turn on those feminine wiles.
(yip-yip-yip-yip-yip-yip-yip)

I'll paint on a Tangee smile
and some glamorous lies.
I'll arch an ebony brow
over heavy-lidded eyes.

29

A scarlet-tipped hand
I'll plant on my hip
while running a pointed tongue
over my lower lip.
I'll put your puny self-control
through a rigorous test;
I'll grab your paisley tie
and improvise the rest.
(I'm so good at improvisation.)

By God,
(diddy doo-wop)
I'm gonna getcha.
(diddy doo-wop)
I'm gonna turn on those feminine wiles.
(yip-yip-yip-yip.)

MARGIE DeMERELL

Like,   Am I Noticed

I   kind of   got my hands on
one of those slick
leather jackets
and   a mean   sort of
cool brown hat
I was just
kind of
walking down the street
sort of
minding my business

30

I felt like
you know,   this . . .
urge to be noticed,
kind of
I   sort of   casually walked
down the street
you know
to the corner
This group of
like
kind of like   cool kids were
sort of   there
I   like   slipped by in
kind of like   a
cool manner
I sort of   wondered
like
if they noticed me
I   kind of   turned around
only to find them   like
laughing at me
I was
sort of   like
really embarrassed   kind of
I   kind of, like
you know
went home

MIKE BELANGER

Sea Sing

Sea sing
your song
of sleep
to us
while in
the high
black sky
white wisps
are whisked
at will.
Sea sing
your song
of sleep
to us.
The dark
blue waves
do purr
and lull
and roll
us down
to peace.
Oh sing
sweet sylph
your song
of sleep.

HEATHER NOYES

The kind of language in which a poem is written can be
the most important part of the poem. For example, the kind of
language can affect how much the reader is willing to read the

poem and, most important, whether the reader believes the poem. For example, a poem written with a lot of words you don't understand isn't going to hold your attention for long. And what chance would the poet of such a poem have of convincing you of his or her sincerity? You might think the poem is phony, that the poet is hiding his or her real feelings behind a lot of fancy vocabulary.

Most of us don't use formal language in our everyday life. We are used to everyday language, which is also called informal or idiomatic. By the way, the word idiomatic is close in meaning to the word "slang." Another word is "vernacular," which also means common speech. Informal language may be the best language for you to write your poems with because it is natural to you. It is the way you most frequently express yourself. Writing essays does not usually allow you to do this. Essay writing requires formal language, at least more formal than the language of poetry. Poetry makes no restrictions on the kind of language you use. It is your choice how formal or how idiomatic you make the language of your poem. For fun, try a poem like the ones in this chapter.

The first poem in the chapter, "Request to a Minstrel," was written by Andrea Cox as a freshman at York Central School in Retsof, New York, in 1981. James Farrer wrote "Seashore Girl" as a senior at McCallie School in Chattanooga, Tennessee, in 1982. James said that his poems come to him "through a chance play on words that develop into a series of images." Margie DeMerell said, "I generally write one or two rough drafts, which I develop as I go along." Margie wrote "You Haven't Got a Prayer" in 1983 as a senior at Lakeland High School in Milford, Michigan.

Mike Belanger wrote "Like, Am I Noticed" as a freshman in 1982 at Carter School in Warren, Michigan. Heather Noyes wrote "Sea Sing" as a senior in 1981 at Goffstown Area High School in Goffstown, New Hampshire. An admirer of Robert Frost, Heather said that she takes her inspiration from nature.

33

"As I start the poem, I have only a vague idea . . . only the emotional impact that I wish to convey."

All of the poets in this chapter have a good ear for language. They like to fool around with words, with phrases, just as a painter likes to play around with line and color. These poets *hear* their poems as they write them. They may even start their poems before they know what they are going to write about. Some of the poets even said this: They don't need a specific subject; they need only the language, a bunch of words or phrases that they like the sound of.

The danger of this kind of writing is that the poet never does establish a subject, leaving the reader groping for what the poem is about. The poets in this chapter escaped this problem. They clearly established a subject and still stuck to their particular kind of language. Some of these poems are very funny. Look at Mike Belanger's "Like, Am I Noticed." This clever, well-done poem ends on a funny note: "kind of, like/you know/went home" — a well-placed joke that the poet makes at his own expense. How easy it would have been to write the poem from the point of view of "he" instead of "I" so that the poet could have protected himself. Yet, how much better a poem it turned out to be because the poet chose to write from his own point of view.

Here is another way to use language as the primary force of a poem: run two voices through the poem at the same time.

Backyard Dreams

looking out over the silent garden
the wind carries the voices
cinderella dressed in
of the children who adored
yella went upstairs to kiss a
this place only yesterday

fella made a mistake
but are now adults who will not remember
and kissed a snake so how
the empty tree weeps and
many doctors did it take
the faded ball is motionless as
one two three four
the grass leans to listen
aw too bad
yearning to hear the memories
you're out

ALLEEN BARBER

Poet Alleen Barber makes it clear that there are two different voices in the poem by writing the second voice in italics. Did you happen to read just the italicized lines? If you didn't, try it. . . . A little poem in itself, right? A funny little song, a song of little kids playing, set against the other voice, the non-italicized lines of the poem, the voice of adults looking back on these times of childhood. It's an interesting way to create a poem. You might try writing a poem like this. You don't have to italicize the second voice. You might indent. You might capitalize. You may indicate a second voice anyway you want — or not indicate it at all, just let the two voices run together. If the two voices are distinctly different, there will be less chance for confusion.

Poet Alleen Barber said, "I got the idea for 'Backyard Dreams' while I was supervising preschool children playing in the playground." Alleen has been active in music since the age of seven. She wrote this poem as a freshman in 1983 at J. M. Alexander Junior High School in Huntersville, North Carolina.

[Untitled]

Walking home from the busstop
I am a magnet for the rain.
Bare-naked worms look like opalescent
squirming noodles in the slinking mud
and I try not to be profound
and think of how they will fry
when the sun shines, Nellie.

A tulip's broken stem bleeds
its crazy flower blood
onto my appalled hand and I'm crying.
no
don't think about sweet sixteen and spring fever
don't think about girls who speak musical phrases
    and dissolve into giggling scarves
     of lavender
        aqua
        mint
        lemon
        and female pink
    when singing of the PROM
don't think about wanting to chew up a whole bouquet
   of them.

Don't dwell on coltish boys, shy and lowbrowed
or handholding
or whirling swipes at the dance floor;
left hand on his shoulder, right hands entwined
the giddy challenge of following his lead.

His breath is soft as dusty pussywillows
on my neck just behind my ear
as I splash, heavily earthbound
into a strategically placed puddle.

MADELYN DETLOFF

Madelyn Detloff generates a lot of wonderful energy in
this poem. She has to be having a good time doing it. I like the
way she works in the song line "When the sun shines, Nellie."
I love the line about chewing up a whole bouquet of flowers.
And the next line is terrific! "Don't dwell on coltish boys, shy
and lowbrowed."

A suggestion about punctuation: be consistent. If you don't
want to use it, then don't. If you want to use it in just one place
in the poem, realize that the place is going to get a lot of notice
because of the punctuation. If you do want to use punctuation,
then be consistent. Try not to punctuate one way in one part
of the poem and then another way or not at all in another part
of the poem because this may confuse the reader.

The same goes for capitalization. Be consistent. If you capitalize in only one place in the poem, you bring a lot of attention
to that place, perhaps more than you want. There is one particular thing about capitalization in poetry that you may have
noticed. There is the convention in poetry of capitalizing the
first word of each line. Some poets like this convention. Obviously, if you want to use this convention, stick to it throughout.

Punctuation and capitalization in poetry are there to as-
sist, not to be noticed. You can use them to show the reader
how to read your poem. Punctuation, capitalization, and spac-
ing are signaling devices.

5
Imagery, Simile, Metaphor

Perhaps you have heard the term "imagery." It is related to the word "image," which usually means something you see, real or imagined. And, yes, "imagine" comes from the same root.

Imagery in a poem is anything in the poem you can experience through your senses. It can be a description of something visual, but an image may also represent a smell, a taste, something you can touch, or even an internal feeling such as drowsiness or hunger.

A Dancer's World

She stands
tall, proud,
reflections of herself
in the four mirrors;
her pointed toes are strong,
and her scuffed slippers
    show a lifetime of dedication.
she extends a leg,
    reaching, tense,
and a softly curved arm in a pink leotard
    leads her to wander
even if only to another mirrored corner.

TIFFANI TENNISON

Tiffani Tennison wrote this poem in 1981 as an eighth-grader at Classical Junior Academy in St. Louis, Missouri. "A Dancer's World" is a descriptive poem. There are lots of words in Tiffani's poem that describe things we can see. In fact, her poem is mostly a physical description. Therefore, "A Dancer's World" is full of imagery.

The naming of real things and using physical descriptions are the simplest ways of establishing imagery in a poem. Imagery does not necessarily make for a better poem, but the more imagery there is, the more the reader can "see" what the poem describes.

On the Beach

I am lying on a towel
Soaking up the summer sun.
Soft grains of sand sheathe my feet.
Starving gulls soar and drop to my side.
Demanding and commanding,
The gulls gaggle together.
"We want, we want!" they seem to scream
Like a spoilt child on a grown-ups' Sunday.

JULIET GAINSBOROUGH

Juliet Gainsborough has a poem earlier in this book. Juliet said, "The poems I have written have all developed from discussions on concrete details in a creative writing class. For instance, the idea for the poem 'On the Beach' came when we imagined going on a trip to the beach."

Juliet develops her poem much the way Tiffani Tennison developed hers: She adds one physical detail to another to build a picture (an image) of being on the beach. Both poems are physical descriptions — but Juliet does a few additional things. Instead of saying "soft grains of sand cover my feet," she writes "soft grains of sand sheathe my feet." "Sheathe" is not the predictable word here. It is more expressive, particularly if you like the idea of feet being "sheathed" as one might sheathe a sword. By choosing to use this word, the poet is suggesting there are similarities between a foot and a sword. The sound of the word "sheathe" is expressive, too.

Juliet creates a similarity later in the poem in another way. Do you hear it? She writes " 'We want, we want,' they seem to scream," speaking of the gulls. Obviously a scream is something we think of a person doing — not that other animals can't scream. The point is that the poet is suggesting that two very different things — sea gulls and people — can seem similar.

Juliet uses another technique to suggest a similarity. It occurs in the last line. Did you notice? "Like a spoilt child on a grown-ups' Sunday." The word "like" compares the sea gulls' screaming to "a spoilt child on a grown-ups' Sunday." Do you happen to know what a similarity created by using the word "like" is called? A "simile." This term isn't particularly hard to remember. Similarity, simile. Simple.

Prejudice

Prejudice is like the feeling you get
When you're left out of a game
It is like the music of
A seashell: hollow and distant
It's when you never reach the front door;
Always being turned away at the first step.

KIMBERLY HARMON

"My poem 'Prejudice' was based on what blacks and other minorities have to go through," wrote Kimberly Harmon as an eighth-grader at Brookwood Junior High School in Glenwood, Illinois, in 1982. This poem is noteworthy for what the poet has done to the idea of "the music of a seashell." Usually, the sound you hear when you press your ear to a shell is thought of as lovely — the sound of the sea. But Kimberly says it is "hollow and distant" — wonderfully descriptive words for what prejudice feels like.

It's interesting that Kimberly doesn't just write "the sound of a seashell." By writing "music" instead of "sound" she sets the reader up for a positive expectation — then reverses and expresses the feeling as negative, as "hollow and distant."

41

Kimberly builds her poem from a series of comparisons. There are three of them. Do you see them? The first two similes are two lines long. The third one is a little different from the other two. Do you see the little shift? Instead of "like" Kimberly uses "when." This implied simile is called a "metaphor," and will be discussed later in the chapter. The word "as" can also be used to create a simile.

My Blind Heart

My heart is like a moth . . .
It flies blindly about
And then it lands
In the perfect spot,
Only to be whisked away
By the emotionless wind,
To search for something new
That can be loved as much.

CHARLENE DUNLAP

Do you see the simile here? It's right there in the first line. An insulting question, right? Well, let's try a harder question: How does this poem differ from the others we have read in this chapter in its use of simile? If you say that the whole poem is a simile, you are absolutely right. The poet states the simile in the first line, and then keeps expanding on the idea of the simile, the heart as a moth. The whole poem is the simile. A simile of more than a couple of lines is often called an extended simile.

Charlene Dunlap wrote this intriguing poem in 1983 as a sophomore at Oelwein High School in Oelwein, Iowa.

Magenta

Magenta is the taste of cherries on a cool evening:
   raspberries in a purple bowl,
   a sunset over the summer tide,
   the fragrance of a rose at dawn.

Magenta is the grating of water on a rock:
   the winding motion of a waterfall,
   luscious strawberries that melt in the mouth,
   an aroma of cake and tea leaves at six.

JULIET GAINSBOROUGH

    There are two ways to suggest a similarity between one thing and another. You know about simile. In a simile, the similarity is established by the word "like." If the word "like" (or "as") is left out and the similarity is suggested, or implied, rather than stated directly, you have what is called a "metaphor." Metaphor is an implied similarity, or comparison. "Magenta is the taste of cherries on a cool evening" is a metaphor. The similarity between the color and the taste is made without using "like" or "as."
    You could say that there isn't much of a difference between simile and metaphor, that they are two terms for basically the same thing, and you would be right. Sometimes, though, the difference can be dramatic.

Sadness

A cube
Tumbling quietly
In the dark

DAVID AWL

The poet might have said "sadness is like a cube," but instead he uses a metaphor to suggest the similarity. His omission of the words "is like" contributes to the strange and lonely feeling the poem creates. David Awl wrote "Sadness" in 1983 as a junior at East Peoria Community High School in East Peoria, Illinois. "Magenta" was written by Juliet Gainsborough, who also wrote "On the Beach" in this chapter and "Cheddar Cheese and Chocolate Cake" earlier in the book.

The simplest image is a physical detail or physically descriptive word. The more complex images are similes and metaphors. They are more complex because they involve a connection, a stated or implied similarity.

Try a poem in which you use a couple of kinds of imagery. Don't worry about what to write about. Just start with physical words and see what they suggest in your imagination. Then write down your thoughts about the technique of imagery. Did you like using it? Does it stimulate your imagination?

Associations

Clouds

A scampering scoundrel,
    an impertinent child,
    a meddlesome lovebird,
    a hunting cheetah.
A cloud is a spider,
    creeping
    on the ceiling.

The unclean wool of unshaven sheep
    a gossamer scarf
    on the necks
    of the peaks,
a dark collage of colors,
    a splatter of white paint.

A cloud is a teenager
    shrugging off the sun,
    the moon,
    the stars,
    to join its scandalous clique.

HELEN GARDNER

Helen Gardner wrote "Clouds" as a freshman in 1982 at Greece Olympia Senior High School in Roch, New York. Helen wrote her poem after watching clouds flow over the lake where she had been sailing. Helen Gardner used the writing method of free association: She looked at the clouds and opened her mind to whatever the shapes suggested. Then, as you can see in the poem, she simply stated the associations. Free association is a fun way to write a poem. Give it a try. Here is another example of free association writing.

White

Ice crackling like a rifle shot,
A bridal gown, crisp and lacy,
The fog, cold, enveloping,
A tiny ghost hiding behind a tree and giggling,
A shimmering waterfall,
    White

ALIETTE SCHEER

Aliette Scheer also uses the method of free association. Aliette wrote this color poem as an eighth-grader at Harding Township School in New Vernon, New Jersey, in 1981. I like the "tiny ghost" in the poem "White." Aliette said, "The color poems were poems where I described what came to mind when I thought of the colors through each of my senses." Aliette's method of free associating through each of her senses is one you might want to try. You never know what you are going to come up with.

The method of free association doesn't have a lot of rules, but it does have an anchor; it begins with a subject. You free-associate *from* something — a color, for example. But what if you drop that anchor and just go from one association to another? There is a term for this. It is called "stream of consciousness." Simply put, the term means writing what comes into your mind. This could turn out to be gibberish. On the other hand, it might turn out to be pretty interesting. When you just open up and stop worrying about what comes out, the results can surprise you. Besides, stream of consciousness is writing you can do fast. In fact, you *should* do it fast in order to maintain the quick movement from association to association. Here is an example.

Suzy Lynn

I named you proudly
what a beautiful rag doll
yarn hair of course
long dress, laced pantaloons
a bonnet and hair ribbons
    to match
and the perfect white
    (but now gray)
apron modestly displays
"Flora, Indiana 1872–1972"
my grandmother's home
    (quilts, clocks, and
    shaded lilies-of-the-valley)
in that clump of a town
that just as proudly
    celebrates centennial
as spring rejoices its earth
or a mother the coming
    of her child
with fireworks and floats
    and the mayor in a car

I sat on the curb
       and held your hand
its seams now burst
       leaking dust-pulled cotton
you smile serenely back

JULIE BENTLEY

Julie Bentley wrote "Suzy Lynn" in 1981 as a senior at Bowling Green Senior High School in Bowling Green, Ohio. About this poem Julia said, " 'Suzy Lynn' is almost verbatim stream of consciousness. ["Verbatim" means "in the exact words."] I try to write for half an hour every night before I go to bed to 'keep in shape.' One night I felt particularly uninspired and ended up writing about a rag doll propped up on my bed. What started as a physical description led to memories associated with the doll and finished as one of my favorite poems."

You might not see much difference between stream of consciousness writing and writing by free association. Julie Bentley said that she began with the rag doll by her bed. Isn't this basically the same as beginning with, say, a color? The only difference is that free association is a series of associations related to *one* specific subject, whereas in stream of consciousness writing you don't go back each time to the subject but, instead, you keep going from the previous association. Stream of consciousness writing is a string of associations. Do you have a preference? Have you ever written in stream of consciousness style? Some people write this way in their journals. Some of the poems in this book may have developed from this wide-open, associative kind of writing.

We have read examples of writing by free association. There is another kind of writing by association. It is called "allusion."

48

"Allusion" means "reference." The poet "alludes," for example, to another poet or poem within his or her own poem. In the next poem, poet Lisa Rabin alludes to both a poet and a particular poem. You may have read the original poem and heard of the poet.

Reflections in Frost

Something in her that never loved a mirror
Would snap the light-beams out upon them both,
And look her over cross-eyed in the dark,
And leave shower steam to percolate there.
Regarding others was another thing:
The girl peered into cracks of glass eyes
When she caught them alone with their blinds up.
But peeping didn't reflect her at all.
He did that. Only a few times she shared him
Filled with blond warmth on an afternoon surf
After a swell. He followed himself gently
As the crest rose, frost with live sea
As the stir crazed and claimed his force.
Soon she caught the fresh backwash of his wave,
Swinging over its gentle peak to the sand.
Such flakes of shore confetti they threw aloft
She knew her inner mirror had fallen.
He winked in shared whimsy, it seemed to her,
Sea crystals adrift on his cool, blond brows
Like salt sprinkled over warm, brown pretzels.
Later, she only half-wished to return
With him. Inside was the first place to look:
Nowhere else was she likely to be stronger.

So after climbing out of the shower,
She blew vapor away on the mirror,
TOWARDS its edge, till the glass could bear no more,
But gulped the woman and framed her with frost.
She could do worse than be a watcher of mirrors.

LISA RABIN

Perhaps you recognize the allusion. This means, perhaps you recognize the reference in Lisa Rabin's poem. Do you know the poet? It is Robert Frost, the modern American poet. And the poem being alluded to is "Mending Wall" by Robert Frost. The first line of Frost's poem is "Something there is that doesn't love a wall." Look at the first line of Lisa's poem. Do you see how she is working off the Frost line?

Is this copying? Couldn't this be called plagiarism? Copying occurs when the writer *doesn't* acknowledge his or her source. Allusion is the opposite. Allusion freely admits the source. In fact, the writer *hopes* that the reader knows the source well enough to recognize the reference to it. By alluding to a poem by Robert Frost, Lisa Rabin hopes to reinforce her own ideas with those of the other poet. She makes sure she establishes the allusion by writing a first line that is very close to the first line of the Frost poem. You may have noticed another way she makes her allusion. Did you happen to notice the title? You see, Lisa has included the poet's name in the title by means of a pun (a play on words).

Clearly Lisa Rabin admires the poem she alludes to in her own poem. Perhaps there is a poem you particularly like. It might be by a well-known poet; it might be by a student. The point is that you like it. Well, why not write your own poem, taking off from the one you like? You will be using the method of allusion in your writing. You will be writing a variation of the poem you admire. The easiest way to allude to the original

50

poem is to mention it in a note just below the title — for example, "after a poem by" and fill in the poet's name.

Lisa Rabin wrote this poem in 1982 as a senior at Will C. Crawford High School in San Diego, California. Lisa said that "Reflections in Frost" is "an ode to Robert Frost's poetry, weaving within it my natural experiences."

Irony and Satire

Dr. Good Blue

blue eyes
so sympathetic
almost crying
for me

and dedicated
must think
very ethical
mr. blue eyes

tall, with son and daughter
framed on desk.
blue eyes too.
crayoned pictures with

so so big blue
eyes.   dr. good blue

NANCY WATZMAN

Nancy Watzman wrote "Dr. Good Blue" in 1982 in her senior year at Northwood High School in Silver Spring, Maryland.

This poem is complex because it says one thing and means another. The poem seems to flatter its subject, the doctor. Yet the poem doesn't feel flattering. The description is too exaggerated to be believable. The reader begins to sense that the poet is poking fun at her subject, even though she never really says so.

Such treatment of a subject is called "ironic." When one overstates an attitude to suggest the very opposite attitude, one is writing in an ironic way. "Ironic" is the adjective form of the noun "irony." If neither word is familiar to you, perhaps you have heard the word "sarcastic" or "sarcasm." Sarcasm is more biting, critical, and obvious than irony.

Satire is a kind of literature that depends heavily on irony. Satirical poems have a particular feeling to them. This feeling is sarcastic, and critical — one of having fun at the expense of the subject.

Another word you can use when talking about the feeling of a poem is "tone." Tone can be defined as the attitude of the poet toward her or his subject. In a satire the poet is being indirect. Therefore, what the poet thinks about the subject may not be altogether clear. The literal meaning of the words expresses one idea and the overall, suggested meaning expresses something very different.

Deer Hunting

First, get a license and a few boxes
of shells. Put your 12-gauge
in the back of your truck
with a shell vest, camouflage jacket and bright
orange hat. Pick up your friends,
find an uninhabited section
of woods and get drunk. You

should hunt in a "flying wedge"
trampling as much as possible.
Shoot at falling leaves, cows,
horses, other hunters, cars,
picnickers and birdwatchers.
Above all, don't be quiet;
that makes the deer suspicious
this time of year.

CHAD ATKINS

Chad Atkins wrote "Deer Hunting" as a senior in 1982 at Interlochen Arts Academy in Interlochen, Michigan. "Deer Hunting" doesn't appear at first to be making fun of anything, at least not until you get down to the last line of the first stanza. Things change, though, in the second stanza: You can tell that the poet is writing a spoof of how to go hunting because everything he says to do is just the opposite of what you actually should do. So the poem is clearly a satire of how not to go hunting.

There is more to "Deer Hunting." The poet knows his subject so well that while writing a satire of how not to hunt he is able to describe how some people actually do hunt. The satirical description fits more hunters than we would like to imagine. These hunters are a danger not just to other hunters who stringently follow all safety guidelines, but anyone nearby. The poem is deadly serious, while appearing to be only a light satire. This combination makes "Deer Hunting" an ironic poem, and a very good one.

Must love always be treated seriously in a poem? What do you think?

[Untitled]

These invoices on my insurance
Are so annoying.
I have been filling out forms
To file a claim for compensation
On a broken heart.

Those inefficient secretaries at the office
Coldly rubber-stamp everything as
"Run-of-the-mill-reject"
And then say, "Next, please."

Somehow I've got the feeling
I am not fully covered
By my present policy.

LIRA TOLLISON

This is fine, tongue-in-cheek writing. The poet has a very light touch. Lira Tollison wrote this poem as a junior in 1983. She attended Warsaw Community School in Winona Lake, Indiana.

Death Wish

I want to experience death.

I want to feel the faltering of my heart
    and its flutter as it comes to a
    tremulous stop.

I want to see the heavy black velvet,
    cloaking and smothering, while I
    choke on my last gulp of air.

I want to feel the paralysis of muscle
    and the last tingle of pain as
    my nerves slowly cease to function.

I want to smell the great heaps of earth
    and her cold, clammy sweat as
    I am entered therein.

I want to hear the resounding echoes
    of nothingness when I have
    nothing to hear but silence.

I want to feel the heat slipping
    from my body as my life
    slowly falls away.

I want to experience death.
    And most of all, I want
    to live to tell about it.

DEANNE PALAS

I admit, I took the poet Deanne Palas seriously about wanting to experience death. She had me convinced. This made the ending all the more of a surprising reversal for me. I was relieved, too. The poet let me off the hook, so to speak. I had been spoofed — and I liked it.

To write this poem, Deanne Palas took off some time from her music, 4-H, drama, softball, and many other activities. She was a senior at M.F.L. Community School in Monona, Iowa, in 1983. The idea of the poem isn't original, which makes its success all the more admirable. Here is what the poet said about the poem: "I always had a taste for things that are a little absurd, and 'Death Wish' is proof of that. . . . [People] are immensely curious about what it's like to be dead, but they don't want to leave life to find out."

Making fun of someone or something doesn't always have to be critical. In fact, it can be done in a loving way. Here is Emily Kolinski as an eighth-grader from Harper Woods, Michigan, writing in 1983 what she called "a slightly exaggerated description."

My Brother's Room

My brother's room, my brother's room,
It's any cleaning person's doom.
My brother's room would be enough
to weaken any cleaning buff.
Under his bed are shoes and socks,
and in his bed are building blocks.
His carpet is all stained and spotted,
his clothes are on the floor, all knotted.
In his drawer you'll find a frog,
and in his closet is the dog.
No respectable mouse or rat
would make his home their habitat.

For in there nothing could survive.
In fact, how can he be alive?

EMILY KOLINSKI

Writing satire, light or heavy, can be fun. Writing ironic poems is a way to pack a lot of feeling into a small space.

8

Fantasy

Fantasy

I think I'm adopted —
A fairy child.
Or a changeling.
I can't be
The child
Of these earthbound
Adults
Who've raised me.
They are
Limited.
I am
Not.
No, I must be from
Another world
Where people
Float
And live their
Dreams.

(I could almost
Believe it
If it wasn't
For my
Nose.)

ELAINE NORMAN

Fantasy poems make up their own reality. They are born in the imagination, and they grow up there. Fantasy has always been popular with artists because the artists need make no concessions to reality. Instead, the artwork may dwell totally in the world of imagination.

What Happens When You Eat Sardines

One day my mother fixed me
some sardines.
I said I didn't want to eat 'em.
But I ate 'em.
They made me sick.

Next morning Mom told me
to eat my sardines.
"That's what got me sick," I said,
but I ate 'em.
The following morning
my legs changed into a fishtail.

The third day,
when sardines
were there on my plate,

I muttered,
"I hate 'em!"
but I ate 'em.
Overnight a dorsal fin
sprouted down the
middle of my chest.

Again
we had sardines for breakfast.
You just can't argue with my mother.
I ate 'em.

I turned into a giant salmon
Before we could say,
"Eat your sardines,"
I dived into the Pacific Ocean,
headed north for Alaska,
and swam out of sight.

LINWOOD WELLS

What I like about this poem is the way it starts off very matter-of-factly and then suddenly shifts to fantasy in the last line of the second stanza: "My legs turned into a fishtail." If this is crazy, how about having sardines at every meal? The whole poem is pretty crazy. I like it. I especially like the line: "You just can't argue with my mother."

Try a poem like this. Start off matter-of-factly, as the poet does here, and then make the jump to fantasy. From there, go wherever your imagination takes you.

Linwood Wells wrote this poem in 1981 as a seventh-grader at Good Shepherd School in Richmond, Virginia.

61

The previous poem, "Fantasy," was written in 1981, too, by Elaine Norman who had another poem appear earlier in this book. Elaine says, "Many of my poems were written as journal entries because my creative writing class has a requirement that we are to keep a journal every day. We are to record our thoughts, feelings, and experiences in any form we wish."

The Oldest Dancers

They are standing
Straight and tall.
Their green and brown skirts
Move and sway
With the wind.
There are many kinds,
Brothers and sisters to one another.
One, tall and stately,
Followed by a wizened old man.
They all ring around a lake
Dancing in their own way
To unaudible music.
They weave a mystic pattern
In the moonlight.
When the wind stops
They stop too and just
Listen.
Then they start their steps again.
When one watches them, they
Look like shadows
Moving.

The wind stops again.
The music stops,
Wavering.
A pink glow comes over the horizon.
Dawn is near.
They dance again
Faster and faster.
The sky is gold,
Creating a ring once more.
They stop,
Scurry to their places.
The sun is up,
The day has begun,
And the dancers are trees once more.

LORI KEYES

Think back to the stories you read as a child, or that someone read to you. Weren't many of them fantasies? And how did
they end? Didn't many of them end with the main character
waking up? This turns the fantasy into a dream. Dreams and
fantasies have a lot in common. Yet there is an advantage to
making a fantasy a dream. The person in the dream can wake
up and return to "normal" life. Otherwise, how does the person
get back to the "real" world? "The Oldest Dancers" feels like
a dream, doesn't it?

Lori Keyes wrote "The Oldest Dancer" in 1983 as an
eighth-grader at Pine Grove Junior High School in East Syra-
cuse, New York. Lori likes fantasy: she cited J. R. R. Tolkien
as one of her favorite writers.

Haven's Green

When I was six,
I saw green
on the TV,

Fire and smoke from the sea-green trees
And men that jumped
From the glass
of the sky,

Blurred green larvae in the grass,
Born from swollen
Green mother
helicopters,

That spilled their loads into the cover
With the other
Quiet stallers,
hid away,

And Walter Cronkite saw it, too,
But he did not see me
As I ran out to play
In the summer green
mimosa tree,

Swallowed by the living leaves,
Tangled in the web of green.

JAMES FARRER

64

In "Haven's Green," James Farrer shows how something as unnatural as war can be transformed by a child's imagination into a series of vibrant and mysterious images.

Childhood is a wonderful time setting for fantasy poems because when we are very young, we live a lot in our imaginations. There are many poems in this book that we could call childhood fantasy poems. Do you remember some of your imaginative ideas when you were a little kid? You might have a fine subject for a poem in these childhood imaginings. It might be fun to try to write one as if you were that age. James Farrer has two other poems in this book.

Fireflies

in this forest a soft somnolence
is dripping from the air and sticks
on hot black leaves

unlit by a moon, the trees
are lonely without their shadows' yawns
and murmur a vague discontent

whatever grows in the dark
explodes with nightloved flowers that heal
the forest's unfilled spaces

(sleepwalker, your transit through this
mysterious land is by memory
pulsing with echoing loons)

on the road the fireflies burst
briefly
glowing in random groups
and etching a furtive humour

they burn with a secret fire
like candles under water

ROBERT STRAZDS

I see Robert Strazds's poem "Fireflies" as a partial fantasy poem. It makes some use of a realistic scene and then goes quickly into fantasy. Robert begins in a forest and then uses the freedom of fantasy to develop a scene with a rich and intriguing mood.

In writing a fantasy poem, usually it is a good idea to establish early on in the poem that this is the world of the imagination. The reader needn't worry about the way things are in the real world because in fantasy everything is possible. Sometimes, though, the poet doesn't admit to writing a fantasy poem. Instead, the poet tries to make the poem seem realistic. That way, when the fantasy part comes in, it has a dramatic impact. The reader is surprised and, for a moment at least, confused as to what might be real and what might be fantastic. This is an interesting kind of poem to write because it allows you to get your feeling across in a powerful way. Here is an example.

Jewelry Store

The sky stretches,
awful and beyond me.
The sun cuts sword slashes at my eyes
so I see none
of the purple front-yard vinca.

Comfortable
to come in for awhile,
away from the sky. I lean
on a display case, almost touching
shelves on either side
and behind me the open door.
The woman at the counter
sits plump in the softening shadows,
dressed in black,
winking gold chains around her neck
reflected in the display cases.

The jewelry on the shelves is also gold,
like sunlight caught
and twirled into bracelets, rings, necklaces.
One is what I want.
I toy with it,
run it through my fingers,
and it coils, scaled and glinting
like a snake. The woman sees
my smile and my purse
and she knows how it glitters. Yes,
I will buy it.

But as I reach for change
the doorstop slides,
and slowly, hissing,
shuts out sun and sky,
gold tarnishes, the woman grins,
shows her teeth, grabs my wrist,
her black dress
and the shadows
fill the room. . . .

I catch the door in time. Outside,
the scorching, spreading sun and sky still hurt.
But kneeling beside the vinca,
nourished by this sun and sky,
I laugh aloud
with the untarnished, painful sun.

ELIZABETH ALLEN

This is a strange poem. Are we reading a realistic poem?
Are we reading a poem that mixes reality and fantasy? What
do you think? And what do you think in general about the way
fantasy can cut in and out of everyday life?

Elizabeth Allen wrote this poem in 1983 as a junior at
Germantown Academy in Fort Washington, Pennsylvania.
Elizabeth worked on the school newspaper and literary magazine, as did many of the poets in this book. Richard Wilbur
and Elizabeth Bishop are her favorite poets.

9
Lyric Poems

Fantasy

I wish
    I could construct
    a colossal web
    sweeping across
    starry heavens
    to ensnare the
    morning dew
    to illuminate your
    day.

RODNEY CAULDER

You have probably heard the term "lyrics," meaning the words of a song. Sometimes, people say "song lyrics." The meaning is the same. You may know of songwriting teams in which one person writes the music and the other writes the lyrics.

Have you heard the term "lyric" to mean a kind of poem? The word has this meaning, too. A "lyric" or "lyric poem" is a short, usually positive poem, often about nature. The meaning of lyric in poetry and in music are related. They are both rooted in song. "Lyric" is the most songlike kind of poetry. In fact, many lyric poems sound like songs, and some have been put to music.

A primary source of poetry is song. Creating a song and creating a poem arise from the same desire: to express a feeling. Both use words. Song lyrics are meant to blend with the music. A lyric poem makes use of the music of the language.

"Fantasy" is a lyric poem. It is short, positive, melodious, and draws on nature. Many lyric poems are expressions of intense personal emotions such as love, just as many songs are about love.

What distinguishes one lyric poem from another is the way the poet makes use of the language. Usually, the poet does what Rodney Caulder does in "Fantasy." He or she reaches for strong images from nature and tries to deliver these images as musically as possible. In short, writing a lyric poem means drawing on the visual and musical possibilities of the language to convey a simple point.

The same is true of a love song, the only difference being that the words, the lyrics, don't have to carry the expression entirely because the music does that, too. Still, the lyrics can contribute a lot to the beauty, power, and excitement of a love song.

Can you think of another place where poetry and song join together, other than in poems and songs about love? Well, you might think of valentines or other short, popular kinds

70

of poetry. What about the words in greeting cards? Aren't these often in the form of poems? Short rhyming poems have long been a part of greeting cards.

What about children's poetry? Is children's poetry another place where poetry and song meet?

Storms

There will be storms, child
There will be storms
And with each tempest
You will seem to stand alone
Against cruel winds

But with time, the rage and fury
Shall subside
And when the sky clears
You will find yourself
Clinging to someone
You would have never known
But for storms.

MARGIE DeMERELL

This poem is addressed *to* children, and the poem takes on an important, scary subject: being alone. What's wonderful about the poem is the way it expresses an important truth in a surprising way: When you are scared and feel alone, you will come to know well and in a loving way someone "You would have never known/ But for storms." This is a reassuring poem expressing a major point in a simple, lovely way. This poem could be set to music.

As close as this poem is to song, it is nevertheless not what we generally think of as children's poetry.

71

Father and Daughter

Father and Daughter
Went out to dine.

They went out to dine
at half-past nine.

At half-past nine
They went out to dine.

Father drank water
And Daughter
Drank wine.

KYLA BOYSE

Isn't this poem more like what we think of as children's poetry? This poem is easier to *say* than the previous poem. It is more fun to say, because the language is playful. Nursery rhymes use playful language. They are fun to say and fun to hear. Many nursery rhymes are soothing — good for putting children to sleep. Many are highly rhythmic — good for singing while playing a game. You might enjoy writing a poem that sounds like a nursery rhyme.

Rodney Caulder wrote "Fantasy" in 1981 while in the ninth grade at Scotland High School in Laurinburg, North Carolina. Margie DeMerell had an earlier poem in this book.

Kyla Boyse composed "Father and Daughter" on a long trip by car. A science-fiction fan and a mystery buff, Kyla said she admires Tomie dePaola and Madeleine L'Engle. Kyla wrote her poem in 1981 as a seventh-grader at Jane Addams Junior High in Royal Oak, Michigan.

Rhyme

An important link between poetry and song is rhyme. And when we say rhyme, we mean more than words that repeat a sound, like "snow" and "crow." We mean a pattern of rhyme. This pattern is of line-ending words, and by pattern we mean a particular sequence of repetition. For example, think of song lyrics printed out on the back of a record album. The rhyming words are at the ends of the lines, and the rhyming forms a pattern. Here is a poem set in a rhyming pattern:

Keep Smiling

Flipping and flopping on the mat,
twisting and turning to shed the fat.
Improve your routine before the meet;
to win first place would be quite a treat.

Remember to smile to the very end,
you want that judge to be your friend.
Salute the judge before you begin;
no mistakes now if you want to win.

The floor exercise is your first event;
make sure your arms and legs are not bent.
The music starts, you do your run.
Make sure you look like you're having fun.

After floor we march to the beam,
it's a lot more difficult than it might seem.
You watch your teammates show their talents,
as they leap and turn trying to keep their balance.

Points will be subtracted for a slip or a fall.
It's also embarrassing, so stay on the ball.
Keep smiling it's not over yet!
You've got to smile, now don't forget.

It's time for you to mount the beam,
if you score high it will help your team.
You did your routine without a mistake.
That certainly is a lucky break.

The meet moves along, it does not halt.
Now it is time for your team to vault.
Run with full speed and do your trick,
and when you land make it stick.

If you get good height and run full steam,
you may score higher than on beam.
Your smile is getting a little thin,
widen it up into a grin.

That's the way, you hit it well,
you should score high but it's hard to tell.
The uneven bars are your last test,
and you really want to do your best.

You chalk your hands to strengthen your grip,
it also helps prevent a rip.
You jump and glide on the bar,
with hopes of being an Olympic star.

You kip from the bottom to the top,
then you gracefully do your drop.
You dismount with a smile on your face,
sure that your team has won first place.

JULIA BROWNE

Julia Browne wrote "Keep Smiling" as a seventh-grader
at Brownel Middle School in Grosse Point Farms, Michigan,
in 1983. "In my poem I describe the four events I work on for
my gymnastics." Clearly Julia knows her subject well. It's no
wonder that Julia especially admires international gymnast
Cathy Rigby. Julia Browne makes it clear in her poem how
much work gymnastics is. Still, the poem reads as if she loves
her training and enjoyed writing the poem. Here is another
poem set in a rhyme pattern.

My Undergrad

Just some jumpy little guy with greasy
Black shoes, who's into varsity track
and Campus News. He dances like a
madman out on the cruise, but he's slick
As ice and twice as smooth. O the bounces
so high that his feet belie. He's
Just a jumpy little guy from his hat
to his shoes. And he's cool, so cool.

JENNIFER RUDIO

Do you see a rhyme pattern in the poem "My Undergrad"?
Rhymes at the ends of lines are called external rhymes. Rhymes
that occur within lines are called internal rhymes. "My Undergrad" was written as an internal rhyme assignment.

Jennifer Rudio wrote "My Undergrad" in 1983 as a senior
at Hellgate High School in Missoula, Montana.

It's fun to fool around with rhyme. Actually, rhyme is a
good way to get a poem started when you don't have anything
in mind to write about. Just pick some rhyming words, set
them in some sort of pattern, and write lines into the rhyming
words. The lines may not make much sense at first, but you
may find a subject you like, something you hadn't thought of
before. Then you can either try to keep the subject in the rhyme
scheme or, if the rhyme pattern is getting in the way of your
expression, drop the rhyme scheme and let the poem find its
own form.

California Man

If I could just refute the L.A. rush
And go flex upon those steel and iron plates
And feel the flush of blood and the crush
Of my flesh under the crush of the weight,
I'd grow to where the beach would feel me,
To where the fleshful eyes of Venice sands
Would turn their grasping gaze and peel me
To a statue with their practiced hands,
And I would know those sun-flaked beauties then
And feel their bronzed ski-sloped breasts
Breathe their sleepy female sighs that thin
The smoggy night upon a soft request.
I'd join the muscled giants by the clanging street
Where they stack themselves like slabs of salted meat.

JAMES FARRER

James Farrer is working in a specific rhyme form (also called a rhyme "scheme"). This form is called a "sonnet." A sonnet is a 14-line poem of patterned rhyme. There are different kinds of rhyme schemes for different kinds of sonnets. The rhyming words in "California Man" fall into this pattern: *ababcdcdefefgg,* where each letter stands for a different rhyming sound. This is the rhyme scheme for a Shakespearean sonnet, popularized by William Shakespeare. More important, though, is simply that the sonnet form is a popular challenge with poets.

Many sonnets are love poems. James Farrer is working in this tradition, too, but with an original twist. Instead of addressing his love to one woman, extolling her beauty above all other women and asserting his loyalty, James envisions himself as a muscular, tanned guy on the California beaches, adored by all the girls. That may sound like the subject for a song by the Beach Boys, but this poet brings powerful language to bear on this love fantasy.

We have seen James Farrer's work before with "Seashore Girl." By the way, James Farrer is not from California, but he knows those beaches. He speaks, for instance, of "Venice sands"; Venice is a popular beach town on the southern California coast.

You might think that the sonnet rhyme scheme is about as hard as any you might choose to try to work with, but there is a harder one. Look at the pattern of the next poem.

My Hamster Is a Little Like a Bear

My hamster is a little like a bear.
This comes from having so much fur, I guess.
His antics always beckon me to stare.

His tiny stub of tail is without hair.
And, although small in size, I must confess
My hamster is a little like a bear.

He is bearlike when hiding in his lair,
And, though he leaves his little nest a mess,
His antics always beckon me to stare.

His hindquarters are shaped just like a pear.
He responds with his teeth to my caress.
My hamster is a little like a bear.

He'll wash his ears and groom himself with care.
(A certain vanity he does possess.)
His antics always beckon me to stare.

His small, compacted body is quite fair.
My hamster is a little mouse, unless . . .
My hamster is a little like a bear.
His antics always beckon me to stare.

SHARON FINLEY

This poem is a "villanelle." A villanelle is a poem with both a rhyme scheme and a pattern of particular lines repeating. A villanelle is made up of six stanzas of three lines each except for the last one, which is four lines.

Let's see if we can construct the rhyme pattern. I am going to use a vertical line to indicate a break between stanzas and use letters to represent the line-ending sound. Here is the pattern I come up with for this villanelle: *aba/aba/aba/aba/abaa.*

Besides the rhyme, there are the repeating lines. Which are they and what are their repeating patterns? Line 1 repeats as line 6, line 12, and line 18. Is there another line that repeats? There sure is. Line 3 repeats as line 9, line 15, and line 19 (the last line). So you could say that the line repetition pattern of a villanelle involves two lines, the first and third, each repeating three times at specific points.

Let's just think for a moment how hard this pattern is to work with. It's hard enough just to write a villanelle that makes sense. Then, if the reader doesn't know the form, the repetition of the two lines may just seem silly. If, on the other hand, the reader does know the villanelle form, then the reader expects this repetition. So how do you, the poet, keep the reader interested? It's a real challenge.

Sharon Finley wrote "My Hamster Is a Little Like a Bear"

in 1983 as an eighth-grader at League City Intermediate School in League City, Texas. Sharon said, "I get the ideas for my poems from everyday surroundings. I had about two rough drafts for each poem. I wrote quickly as soon as an idea came to me."

11
Love Poems

Where Were You Yesterday?

Yesterday it rained
and I stood out in it
hoping
by chance
that you'd just happen to come outside.
But I knew that if you did come out,
we'd never be like we were before.
Maybe it's a good thing
you didn't come out.
Besides
who comes out in the rain
anymore
just to talk?

HILWATHA STEPHENS

Tonight the Phone

Tonight the phone is warm
and you come soft to me and brush me with your voice.
The timbres caress me gently
and carry me there.

A robin sings.

Listen to the thaw as the ice reaches to the sun
and dies as water a little bit closer.

In the wet air there is a rainbow.

The sky speaks and tonight I listen to the
touch of you.

LISA FREINKEL

Both of these poems are about love. In "Where Were You Yesterday?" Hilwatha Stephens conveys all too well what many of us have felt and thought . . . the pain in the loss of a love.

"Tonight the Phone" turns me right around and makes me feel that whatever the risk, to love is worth it because love is such an incredible feeling. Lisa Freinkel's poem shows us how just the lover's voice is enough to transform the world.

This question of the risk of love goes well beyond poetry, obviously. Yet poetry is a fine art form for expressing the question, whichever side you want to take. What are your thoughts on this question? Is love worth the risk of bitter disappointment and loss if and when the relationship collapses? What you believe depends much on your experience. Still, you needn't have had many loves to have a strong opinion about this subject.

Write down your feelings, your thoughts. If they begin to resemble a poem, fine. If they don't, keep going with them. See where they take you. When you finish, read over what you have written. You may be surprised. This will be your essay on love. Keep it. Maybe read it over again in a few years, and see how you feel about what you have written. Expressing your feelings is very important. If you want to show it to someone, that's fine. It's fine, too, to keep it to yourself. What comes first is the self-expression.

At Beth Levin's Farm, Lewisburg, PA

As we walked along the goat-cropped ridge
I told her that the ridge across from us
Swooping up so fast the trees were tightening to the
     earth
Was almost sound to me, a great booming.

Later, when it rained and we stood in the barn,
The ridge still came to me through an open window:
A god of the burnt orange oat fields, sleeping,
The back slowly heaving up and down in breath.

In the mist I saw clouds gathered in the thighs
Of mountains like the cool way the Romans molded
The sexes of their statues, and I told Beth
Of the time I walked in the trees Pittsburgh pushed

83

Fifty miles away, and how I met a lame horse half-
   blind,
The blind eye cloudy blue, how I stuck a finger in
Its mouth and it bit, not hard enough to break,
And wouldn't let go. How I stood there four hours

Till my father came and waved hands dizzily
In the horse's face and my finger slid out
Of its awe-hung mouth, how we gave the horse a bit
Of sugar. I told Beth this, looking at the ridge.

JOHN SCHULMAN

Do you think this is a love poem?

I think it is. This poem expresses to me a particular power of love, the desire to share your personal thoughts in a more profound way than you have ever done before.

Much of this poem is the poet's description of what he saw and what had happened to him. Yet the poet makes it clear that he is telling all this to Beth. Besides, look at the title. And look at the last line! Isn't he saying all this for Beth?

I really like the last line. I admire so many things about this poem: the way the third line jumps up at us, that fourth line, the sixth, the eighth! I could go on. But I have to mention one tiny detail that shows me how very capable and thoughtful this poet is. In the first line of the last stanza, we expect the word "his" before "hands"; that's the usual way of writing the detail. But John Schulman leaves it out. I can't believe he did so by chance. Look how leaving out the word "his" makes the scene even stranger, more gruesome. And how will Beth respond? Won't she be drawn into what he is saying even more? Isn't that what he wants?

Summer Evening

The locusts will sing soon . . .
they'll burst from themselves,
their wings,
their song into the July night . . .

and you will come
slip into my darkness —
touch my shadows . . .

the cool steel of the yellow lawn chair
is warmed by my tanned legs
and with the rocking of the dock,
I blend silently into the light . . .

KIMBERLY ENGLAND

Did you have to read these love poems to write one of your own? I didn't think so. If you feel shy about writing this kind of poem, and don't want to reveal yourself, you don't have to use the pronoun "I." In fact, it might be easier for visualizing a scene to use "he" or "she," and to write your poem using the third-person pronoun. Or you might make up someone's name. You can alter the facts, too. In poetry you can do anything. The point is to express the feeling you are after. See how much you can pack into a few words.

The first two poems were written in 1982. "Where Were You Yesterday?" was written by Hilwatha Stephens (who has another poem in this book) at the age of fourteen. "Tonight the Phone" is by Lisa Freinkel. As a student at Evanston Township High School in Evanston, Illinois, Lisa wrote, "Let me tell you one thing: Whether you know it or not, your poetry really stems from everyday life." And as for her favorite poet, Lisa writes, "Roethke is the first poet that ever really made me cry over the beauty of an image. His love poetry is just amazing."

John Schulman wrote "At Beth Levin's Farm, Lewisburg, PA" in 1982 as a senior at Taylor Allderice High School in Pittsburgh, Pennsylvania. The previous summer he attended the Pennsylvania Governor's School for the Arts. "I most admire," John wrote, "the Russian poet Osip Mandelstam for his courage . . . for his acts against the Stalin regime."

Kimberly England said she expresses herself through music and drama as well as writing. She listed Ralph Waldo Emerson and Amy Lowell as two of her favorite poets, but added that Emily Dickinson, in particular, fascinated her. Dickinson's "ability to grasp life in all its intensity is impressive," she wrote, and "her ability to share that intensity in her writing is inspirational." Kimberly wrote "Summer Evening" in 1983 as a senior at Ruskin High School in Kansas City, Missouri.

12
Growing Old

Grandma's Gift

Grandma was someone who . . .
    Watched a mountain goat eat her Kleenex
    Hated to shower in the state parks
    Giggled while she talked to the celery
    Refused to set back her watch;
        insisting on lunch at noon though it was only
            ten.

I remember . . .
    A fly on her toe as she slept on the hammock
    Sharing her squeaky guest bed with my sister
    Pinning the hem on her first pair of jeans
    Photographs of the hood taken from a moving car;
        she was passing through the Grand Tetons.

Grandma . . .
    Kept me up to date on our soap operas
    Bought me underwear whenever she found a sale
    Embroidered pillows for my first dorm room
    Passed down her mother's jewelry to me;
        I wear her love around my neck.

KATE MURDOCK

Kate Murdock says that her poem, "Grandma's Gift," "is dedicated to both my mother's and father's mothers. It is filled with fond memories of trips, conversations, and meals together. Theirs is a gift I someday hope to share with others." The temptation in writing a poem such as this is to become maudlin, overly sentimental. "Grandma's Gift" is not maudlin, and the reason for this accomplishment is the poet's capacity to write with imagination and flair. Just the second line is enough to demonstrate this originality: "Watched a mountain goat eat her Kleenex." This is delightfully wacky. And it's not the only such line. The poem is full of them. For me, the poet keeps this pace up throughout the poem and really earns her last line, "I wear her love around my neck." Out of context, this line doesn't make much sense. In the poem, at the very end, it is the right line. Kate Murdock wrote this poem in 1983 while attending Interlochen Arts Academy in Interlochen, Michigan. An admirer of Martin Luther King, Jr., as are many of the poets in this book, Kate is active in music — piano, French horn, and voice.

A Bottle of Memories

The old man sits alone
cross-legged in the old
broken down rocking chair
gazing at the lawn
through thick, wire-framed
bifocals watching
his grandson chase
monarch butterflies
hoping that maybe he
will come sit in his
lap to listen to tales
of by-gone days
bottled-up in the old
man's mind waiting
to be uncorked.

RODNEY CAULDER

Rodney Caulder wrote about his poem, "A Bottle of Memories," that "The words came to me as I thought of my grandfather." Rodney has another poem in this book.

Honani

Inside the cramped Hopi room,
Honani edges near to the coffee-table,
inlaid with broken bits of pottery,
and peers with watermelon seed eyes
into our faces.

From the pocket of his cardigan
he draws a wooden pipe,
smoothed and polished to a rich brown hue
from many years of fondling
by the hands which cradle it now;
hands, nimble and persistent
from years of punching stubborn keys
on an old black Royal.

His face is a mass of wrinkles
like the land he used to till —
soft ridges in the sun-burned sand.
Now he rocks in a chair,
slowly, deliberately,
answering questions which hover about him
like moths around a naked light bulb.
Finally, tired of our questions,
Honani shuffles back over
to the gaily-covered bed,
shoulders sagging like a broken-down cot
that has held one too many passengers.
His passengers:
a drunken son,
a nagging wife,
a summer with no rain.
He eases himself down,
and motions for me to sit next to him.

Outside,
a sparrow beats its sterile wings,
struggling against the relentless desert wind.

The bird,
another speck of nomadic dust
in the current,
falters and gives in.
It lands on a twisted juniper branch,
and waits patiently
for the time of the red wind
to end.

SIBYL FRANKENBURG

Sibyl Frankenburg wrote "Honani" when she was a senior at East High School in Denver, Colorado, in 1982. An admirer of Ray Bradbury, she said she enjoys participating in various sports and studying different languages.

Elegy for Grandma

The blue egg
is warm in my hand.
It had fallen from the birch tree
onto the soft sod
by the pond,

where we sat
and buried
dead birds,
blue veins
under soft fuzz.
We piled white pebbles
from the pond's edge
on their graves.

This egg is blue
as the eyes
you have closed to spring,
to blue birds,
to white pebbles
and to me.

ANGELA HOXWORTH

Angela Hoxworth wrote "Elegy for Grandma" as a junior in 1983 at Interlochen Arts Academy in Interlochen, Michigan.

About "Elegy for Grandma" Angela wrote, "I was very upset when my grandma died. I never knew her but this strange memory remained strong in my mind. She made me realize that being old can be the most wondrous part of human life." I especially like the last stanza of "Elegy for Grandma." The rhythm is lovely.

Poem 2

When the old man died,
An angel came down from Heaven,
And scooped the soul from within the ancient body,
Which sat alone in some forgotten room.

There was no fanfare.
No trumpets shattered the stillness of the room.
No distant choir wove milk-white threads of harmony.
And nothing surprising or unnatural disturbed the
  eternal peace.

There was just an old man,
And an angel,
Floating
Slowly
Up.

ROD BARR

Rod Barr was a junior in 1981 at Indian Hill High School in Cincinnati, Ohio, when he wrote "Poem 2."

Each year, many of the poems submitted to the Scholastic Awards Program have a common theme: growing old. Often the poets have chosen to write about their relationship with an older person they've known. Sometimes the poems express sadness for the loss of a grandparent, like "Elegy for Grandma." Others, like "Honani," paint a portrait of an individual who has been both enriched and eroded by the passage of time.

You may also have strong feelings about your own grandparents. Try expressing these feelings in a poem. You might begin with something simple — perhaps a memory of an afternoon you spent together. Write down as many details as you can think of, and then choose the ones that best express what you want to say.

13
Making a Statement

You have been reading poems by students with an ear for the language. Some of these poets wrote in a particular kind of language. Perhaps they did so because this is the way they "heard" their poems. Other poets wrote in rhyme. Perhaps they had an idea first and then chose to write in rhyme, or they might have wanted to write a rhyming poem from the start. All of these poets are attracted to the musical quality of language. They like to sing with words.

Poetry may also be used to make a statement. People write in order to state their ideas, feelings, and experiences. As far back as history goes, people have gone out of their way to record their thoughts and accomplishments. Painting is one way. Writing is another. Among the modes of writing, poetry is a good choice for this type of recording because it is condensed and highly personal. Many people choose poetry as a means of declaring a general idea about life.

[Untitled]

Sometimes
 We rush forward in our lives
 And try to speed the aging process
 Until we get to a certain point.

And often
 When we get there
 We try to stay there,
 And stop the aging process —
 Until we look back at our silliness.

And usually
 We wish we'd lived our fleeting lives
 Differently.

But sometimes
 It's too late.

KYLA BOYSE

Some poets turn to poetry to state general ideas. They like to philosophize, to talk about far-reaching concerns and beliefs. These poets prefer ideas to music. They are more interested, in other words, in the sense than in the sounds. Kyla Boyse, who wrote "Untitled," is one such poet. Kyla has another poem in this collection.

Other poets have more specific statements to make.

Through Their Eyes

They call it a place
where dead rats, dead cats and people
are treated equally.

They call it a place
where muggings and murders
are commonplace happenings.

They call it a place
where graffiti dwells on walls and buildings
done by the same spray paint
that is missing from the corner store.

They call it a place
where the strong odor of garbage
piled high upon the streets
is considered one of the important factors
that make this place what it is.

They call it a place
where not many work
a place where many are known to be illiterate.

They call it a place
where a small plate of collard greens
makes the perfect Sunday dinner.

They call it a place
where husbands abandon their wives
wives abandon their children
and children abandon their dreams.

They call it a place
where the Saturday activities
are body confrontations and "hangin' out".

They call it a place
where the natural thing to do
is to get into trouble.

This place is easy to get in
but once in
people seldom get out.

This is a place
where the everyday task
is to stay alive.

They call this place the ghetto
the crowded, dirty ghetto.
I call it my home.

LAURIE FLOWERS

Laurie Flowers was an eighth-grader in 1983 when she
wrote her poem "Through Their Eyes." She attended Gesu
School in Detroit, Michigan. An admirer of Martin Luther
King, Jr., Laurie said, "So many times before, I had been driven
through the run-down sections of Detroit, saw the painful suf-
fering lives of the people, witnessed the bitter, emotionless

expressions on their faces. In my heart, I too felt their pain."
Her poem is an accomplishment of the imagination, for she
gives the reader the feeling that she lives in the very place she
is describing — and yet the title makes clear that she is merely
imagining living there.

Here are two more poems by poets who wish to make a
statement. Both poets have appeared earlier in this book.

Outside the Meat Plant's Walls

Head low,
ears pointed,
the calf stands
in the pasture
behind the meat plant.

The cement is not thick enough
to muffle
the sound of steam
sent to cook blood.

The cement is not thick enough
to contain the red haze
coloring the air for miles
each way.

When the blood taste
of the fine powder
covers the calf's tongue,
his eyes film white
and thin as milk.

CHRISTINE MURRAY

98

Reunion

Chimney swifts belch soot
into an already dusty sky
as I stand on the corner
of Burtner and Murdock

near the thorn woods we crawled
through a long time ago.
Across the street, the swamp
sings no more. Can't see red-winged

blackbirds nowadays, only a vast
mud field covered with empty
stares and apathetic faces
of those who never played there.

Steel balls the size of time
raze the left wing of Birdville
Elementary School while its windows
cry on the sidewalks.

KEN KOSTKA

14
Poetry and Art

I want to ask you your opinion about poetry as an art form. You have certainly read enough poems and written enough of your own poems and thought about poems enough to have some strong opinions about poetry.

What would you say is the best thing poetry can do as an art form? In other words, think about other art forms — painting, dance, film, and architecture, for example — and think about the other genres (kinds) of literature: fiction, drama, and non-fiction, to name a few. How do you think poetry measures up against these? Can it do what the others do? Is there anything it can do that the others cannot? Of the things that poetry can do, what does it do best?

Many people feel, for example, that poetry is an especially good art form for expressing feelings. These people say that poetry is truly a personal art form.

I like this idea of poetry as the expression of feelings, but is it what poetry does best? I think I would opt for poetry's capacity to express a lot with very little. I have always been impressed by how much poetry can convey with so few words.

Some people put this idea another way: They say that poetry is the supreme language — or, in other words, it is language at its best. What do you think of this idea?

Here are some examples of poetry that say a lot in just a few words.

Growing Up

I squirm out of
The snake skin
Leaving it behind
For others
To stumble over.

ASHLEY REAVES

I Am More Foliage

than the flower
and will not bloom/but grow
quiet and green
and spread my leaves under the sun.

EDITH LUNDGREEN

"Growing Up" and "I Am More Foliage" both express a strong energy for life.

Ashley Reaves plays the flute and piano. She wrote "Growing Up" in 1983 as a freshman at Hickman Mills School in Kansas City, Missouri. "Two or three drafts" was usually enough, she said, to complete a poem.

Edith Lundgreen wrote that reading fairy tales and Greek and Norse mythology when she was young helped her most to develop her imagination and creative thinking. "I Am More Foliage" is one of her "life confirmation poems, coming from my need to find joy in the world." Edith was a senior at Henley

High School in Klamath Falls, Oregon, when she wrote this poem in 1983.

Do you see how much expression can be packed into a few words? In good poetry there is the sense of immediacy, of things happening quickly, and non-essential words being left out. Often, a scene is created rapidly, with great economy of language. The feeling the scene conveys is called the "mood." Here are some poems that show poetry's strength at creating a distinctive mood.

Five Finger Exercise

I sit in the middle
of the pond
watching silver leaves
fall into the water
around me. My fingers
play carelessly
at my side
as if they were alone
and far from me.
I look down
and find them swimming
under the leaves,
under the ripples of the pond.
Fish
skimming the water,
absorbed by the sun.

BONNIE NEVEL

Locked In

One papery moth
still holds on
to the screen

   where
White threads from
the cottonwood tree
wave like faded streamers
on a summer fan.

Three pearly eggs
clustered on a brittle leaf.

Summer locked in winter's window.

WHITNEY BURRY

Bonnie Nevel wrote her poem "Five Finger Exercise" as a sophomore at Interlochen Arts Academy in Interlochen, Michigan, in 1981. Of her poem, she wrote, "I was experimenting with the 'i' vowel. I had just been to a Robert Bly poetry reading and was very impressed with his work with the one sustained vowel sound."

Whitney Burry wrote "Locked In" in 1981 as a senior at Raytown High School in Raytown, Maryland. Whitney admires poets Marge Piercy, Maxine Kumin, and Denise Levertov. Whitney makes some interesting points about writing. "In every one of my poems I usually spend many hours revising and perfecting. Sometimes I will sit and just wait for ideas to come to me. I don't make quick decisions about what I want to say. Most of my poems are based on what mood I'm in, where

I am and what I see, hear, taste, and touch. I feel it's important to use as many of the senses as I can."

Another strength of poetry is its limitless range of subject matter. While it is true that other arts have a similar range of subject matter, this book certainly attests to the variety of topics poets address in their poems, as well as to the energy that poets can bring to bear on the oddest of subjects. This energy is also an expression of the poet's delight in the endeavor of writing itself. In other words, poems can demonstrate the enjoyment of writing poems. To express this pleasure, poets will even select writing as their subject now and then.

Confusion

Blue scribbles on white —

I peer into the darkness
Fearful of the words that swirl, blur there

Sharp corners hurt me —
Poking —
Jabbing —

I'm pleading
For help —

ASHLEY REAVES

Teach Me

Show me how to hurt
To write from the gut
A thought is confused in my head
Edit, isn't that a bird that just picks up sticks
for his nest?
Please
Prose to me.

LINWOOD WELLS

Writing is not the only art form that poets write about. They may draw from any art for their subject matter. Here are some examples.

Distant Peaches

after a painting by Cézanne

The air rains about me
and I can see
the peaches
in the distance.

I can see the stubble,
I can see the stem:
I can see the peaches
in the distance.

The peaches on the table,
the apples on the chair:
the air rains about me
and through my scattered robes.

I can see the curtains
wrap around a tea-pot,
an impassioned still apple
in the fling of a napkin.

The peaches with the cleft,
the peaches with the groin:
I can see the peaches
on the table through the air.

JOHN SCHULMAN

Photograph

after a line by Laurence Raab

In the photograph of water the sky is lost;
a reflection of silence

and the water drinks itself
until it is empty

and becomes
like the night.

You become the water
and the sky floats to the surface.

If you could only think of nothing.

BRIAN STAKER

Ashley Reaves, Linwood Wells, and John Schulman have
poems that have appeared earlier in this book. Brian Staker
is from Salt Lake City, Utah.

A Word About Writing

For a poem to have a decent chance of being remembered, it has to engage us directly. If it doesn't make its point fairly clear, we aren't likely to choose to read it again, much less suggest to someone else that he or she read it.

For a poem to be remembered, it needs to be fully developed, fully thought through, fully expressive of its purpose. Put it this way: You can't half write a poem and expect it to be vivid and interesting. Nor can you half cook a meal and expect it to be good. Nor can you half plan a house and expect it to come out well. You need to attend to *all* details and then assess the whole thing, maybe twice, maybe three times, to make sure that all details are integrated to your single purpose. A team can't play its best if only a few players give fine, individual performances. All the players on the team must contribute if the team is to have a maximum chance of winning. When something works out well — in sports or in art — it is because the effort is integrated, unified.

When poets praise a poem as a unified expression, they often say, "the poem works well." They mean that all the parts contribute to the whole, that the poem is fully developed, that the poem "comes together."

How good, then, can a poem be? That's not an easy question to answer because we can't measure the quality of a poem as we might measure the length of a home run. We can, nevertheless, respect a poem that has been around for a long time, centuries, for example. A lot of people had to think it's a good poem for it to last that long. That doesn't mean, though, that you have to like it. You might, you might not. The point is, a poem survives in people's memories. If it is in a book, it has a better chance of surviving. Yet a poem in a book that no one reads isn't being remembered in an active way. So if you think a particular poem is worth preserving, suggest to someone else that they read it. Your suggestion is high praise.

Let's say that you have written a bunch of poems you think are pretty good. The first thing to do is not to throw them out. The second thing to do is to go back to them after a while and see if they still read well to you. Remember, you will have changed in the meantime, so don't be too hard on your old poems. Perhaps some of them are still, in your estimation, pretty strong, and you would like to see if you could make them even better. Then read those good poems over again a number of times and try to get back inside the feelings they express. See if there is any way to express the feelings even more strongly. Look for parts of the poems that could be dropped out, without really hurting the poems. As you work to trim a poem down, you will intensify its expression. Look out, though, because you can cut a poem down too much. What's too much, or not enough? That's for you to decide — and possibly a few good readers you really trust. And whatever else you do, check each word carefully. Check it for meaning and sound.

In order to write good poetry it helps to *read* a lot of poetry.

To better understand the poems you are reading, you might want to try writing *about* a poem. A good rule to follow in writing about a poem is to try to respect it as much as you would want someone to respect your poem. What can you say about someone else's poem, other than that you like it or don't like it? Lots. First, you can say what you understand the poem to be about. Then you can say what you see to be the point or feeling the poet is trying to express. In other words, you can identify the subject of the poem and the poet's attitude toward the subject, or its tone. These are the first two questions to ask when you are trying to establish an overall understanding of a poem.

How do you know if your responses to these two questions fit the poem? Just re-read the poem. Once, maybe twice. Does your understanding of the subject of the poem and its tone fit the poem? If they do, as best as you can tell, then you are on solid footing to go on and say more. Besides, in further writing about the poem, you may come upon something that makes you change your mind, if only slightly. If so, go back and re-phrase your opening statements about the subject and the poet's attitude.

What else might you say about a poem? A simple strategy is to describe, from beginning to end, how the poem develops.

Another thing you can do is discuss how the poem makes use of the properties of poetry. Poetry combines music and idea, sound and sense, feeling and meaning. Try to describe how these three pairs of elements all work together to determine *how* the poem "speaks" and *what* it says.

For example, as to the meaning (or content or idea) of the poem, does the poet simply state this meaning or does he or she also use imagery to suggest it? You can go further. Is the imagery of the poem simply a lot of detailing — or what you might call description — or does the poet use simile and metaphor as well? If these terms aren't clear to you, go back to chapter five on "Imagery, Simile, Metaphor."

110

Let's say that the sound of the poem is especially noticeable to you. What can you say about the way a poem sounds? You can describe it just the way you would describe any sound. Perhaps the poem is full of words made up of very soft sounds. Say so. Cite some examples. Say how these soft-sound words contribute to what the poet is trying to express. The same goes for a poem full of short, hard sounds. Point out examples. Perhaps the poet is trying to express fast action or a feeling of anger or courage.

Another quality of sound is rhythm. Is the rhythm fast and jerky? Is it slow and even? Whatever it is, the poet is using the rhythm to help create the feeling or idea he or she wants to express.

Rhyme is a property of sound. Does the poet use rhyme? If so, does the rhyme contribute to the feeling of the poem? Some poets use rhyme to give the poem structure, or form. Rhyme can make a poem easier to read. Rhyme is pleasant to the ear — but too much rhyme may obscure what is being said. Poets try to achieve a balance of the many elements and devices of poetry so each of their poems will be a unified, integrated whole.

Rhyme is not the only device for structuring. The poet chooses the structure that best suits the poem. What is the poem's structure if it isn't set in a rhyming pattern? Where does the poem start? How does it move on? Where does it end? Structure and development are interrelated matters.

An important property of poetry is language itself. What sort of language makes up the poem? Is the language formal? Is it conversational? Is it difficult? Simple? The kind of words in the poem will tell you much about what the poetry is trying to express.

One more property: point of view. Remember, in writing, the term "point of view" means something other than just an opinion. In poetry it refers to who is "saying" the poem. The easiest way to establish the point of view of the poem is to

111

determine if the poem is written in the first person ("I"), second person ("you"), or third person ("he," "she," "it"). How might the point of view relate to what the poet is trying to express? If the poet is trying to express a personal feeling, the poem is likely to be set in the first person. If the poem is an expression of love, the poem is likely to be in the second person. If the poet wants to speak from a slight distance, as in telling a story about other people, the poem is likely to be set in third person.

These properties of poetry help you to *describe* a poem. Poems can be described just as movies and songs and the weather can be described. You might refer to these properties of poetry as a checklist, just to see if you have noticed and commented on whatever you understand the poet to be doing in the poem to make the poem as memorable as possible. And you can use these properties to help you state your evaluation of the poem. For example, you might decide that the language is much too complicated for what you see to be a simple purpose. Or you might find that the metaphors are so interesting in themselves that they detract from the feeling the poem is expressing. Unity of expression, that's your guidepost.

Perhaps the most interesting question for you about poetry has nothing whatsoever to do with the properties of poetry. The question comes up long before the actual writing of a poem and reading of a poem and writing about a poem. This question is; Why does someone write a poem in the first place? Well, why might *you* write a poem? Are there experiences you want to remember and express in a way that is entirely yours? Have you just come upon a wonderful idea and want to write it down? Your writing might take the form of a poem, rather than just a statement. If you just want to "tell about" something, then you would probably choose a kind of writing other than poetry. But if you want to write it in a way that makes other people "feel it" the way you do, then poetry is a good choice.

Some people write poems just because they like to write, and poetry is one good way to write. People who like writing

112

are often curious how an idea or a feeling will take shape on the page. They like that interaction between what is in their heads and hearts and what happens when they seek language to express themselves. Other people just like to see how exactly they can describe something, an experience, or a feeling. Some people use language to fire up their imaginations. They find that once they start writing, they get lots of new ideas. A very important reason to write a poem — or turn to any art form for that matter — is to express one's personal values. To make a powerful, vivid, memorable expression of your own values is deeply gratifying.

Are there other reasons to write a poem? Sure, thousands probably. Do you think there is one reason that stands out as the best?

16
Creative Thinking

This is the last chapter of this book, so I want to show you some poems I particularly like and talk a little about creative thinking.

You probably know that the term "creative writing" means the writing of fiction, drama, and poetry. I wonder if that is a broad enough definition of creative writing for you. Could writing a good letter, for instance, be just as creative as writing a story?

The word "creative" may have a different meaning for each of us. Whatever that meaning is, I believe that there is a kind of thinking — creative thinking — that must come first before we try creative writing or any other kind of creative activity. We may not all agree on exactly what creative thinking is, but I would guess that we all would include in our definition the making of new connections among ideas, and that these new connections make for a new, deeper understanding.

To make these new connections of ideas, creative thinking requires more than just your intelligence, training, and knowledge. It requires, in addition, your imagination, intuition, vision, and willingness to experiment. A willingness to experiment is a willingness to be wrong or to spend a lot of time trying something only to find out that it apparently won't work. At the heart of creative thinking is risk.

I believe that creative thinking is important to reading poems, writing poems, and writing about poems. You can read a poem by just skimming through it, but you are not likely to get much out of the poem. This is not creative reading. On the other hand, you can read slowly, open yourself up to the poem, and let it take you wherever you want to go. The ideas of the poem and your personal associations can take you to many places in your mind. This kind of reading is what I call creative reading. Creative reading is the only way to get everything from a poem you can. Isn't this the way you would like someone to read a poem you had written? You know now from your own poetry writing how much you can put into a poem. Reading a poem with this kind of concentration and imagination is a creative act, too.

Many people might say that writing a poem is easy because you may write anything you want and in any way you want. But I wonder if writing a poem is all that easy. What do you think? You have written enough poems by now to know that the freedom to write anything you want and in any way you choose doesn't necessarily lead to something you like. You may even have had the experience of sitting there and staring at the paper, waiting for an idea to come by. This can be frustrating. And it also can be discouraging to get a wonderful idea for a poem and not be able to get it down on paper the way you want it. Another way people can become frustrated in trying to write a poem is to get an idea, write like crazy, feel great about what they have written, and then read it the next day, fully expecting to like it, only to find that the writing is lousy. At least it *seems* lousy. Excitement turns to disgust. Many drafts of poems and stories end up in the wastepaper basket.

Creative thinking in writing poetry isn't just the imagining of an idea for a poem, or getting the idea and writing the first draft. It is creative thinking that carries you from the first impulse to something that you consider finished. Wouldn't it be nice if this process were a beeline from idea to completed poem? As you know from your own writing of poems, the process isn't usually that simple. You start to write in one place and off the poem goes to another place. Why does this happen? Because the act of writing sets off new ideas. As you start writing, your brain can become so accelerated by new ideas that you can't write fast enough to keep up with them. This problem actually isn't bad because it signals that you have swung into high gear. But all the ideas jumping around make it tough to move from point A to point B. It's best just to go with the rush of ideas and take stock later. The creative thinking that goes into writing a poem has a powerful way of taking off on its own.

There is a second kind of creative thinking that goes into writing poems, and this is the thinking that evaluates what you have on paper as you go along. This is the creative thinking that makes creative decisions. Does what you have written correspond to what you had in mind when you started? If so, is there anything you might want to add or change or take out? If not, if what you have written is a detour from your original notion, do you like it? Do you hate it? And then, do you scrap it and start over again? Do you try to bend it back in accord with your first idea?

This is what revision is all about: choices. Revision isn't just the streamlining of what you write in a couple of drafts. Revision is deciding how to go on, if you want to. Revision is the act of evaluation within the very process of writing. Revision requires creative thinking because you can't simply decide if a word or phrase "sounds good"; you have to weigh your choices against the whole poem. This means both the poem as it exists on paper and the poem you may still have in your head. Revising can become confusing.

Creative thinking in writing poems calls upon all your strengths. You invent and evaluate at the same time. The creative thinking in writing a poem engages you fully.

All the poems in this book display creative thinking. I have saved a group of poems until here, at the end, that display it, I think, especially well.

116

Winter Trees

We make a way through the snow
Just my father and me
And Pennsylvania's woods
stand guard all around
Now I can smell the
winter desolation in the firs
I can hear it in the silence
And the taste is ice in my throat

I sneak a glance at my father
when he takes my hand
He has never done that before
Then I see his eyes and in
their depths of brown
I see a sadness so intense
like a life of love gone bad

Everything here in the night
is just like a black-and-white movie
There is a valley in the distance
crowned with black lace maples
The sky is pure velvet
and the moon's not in sight
I believe the paleness of our faces
is giving off the only light

There's not a sound all around
and I wonder if perhaps
I've gone deaf
Because now I see tears
pouring down his cheeks
and there's not a sob to be heard

I can't even hear my own

I don't have the sky in my dreams
I never asked for more than my father
I thought his presence in the house
would be all we'd ever need

But illusions tumble down
like the leaves on the maples
And the dreams are buried in the snow
Now I can smell the
winter desolation in the
masculine presence beside me
I can hear it in his silence
And the taste is salt in my tears

DENISE OVERFIELD

Counseling at My Old Camp

At camp, in the wooded hills upstate,
we hunted fossil shells and bits of quartz.
Which were older? No one knew.
The seas were long emptied,
the way crystals were made
buried deeper than our trowels could reach.

And if we had known, running to the woods,
that crystals were only the way atoms fell,
would we have cared? Yes, and tall in our knowledge
we would have corrected anyone
who tried to tell us stories of lost girls
and their jewels, and of the world
that lives outside the fire's light.
We knew better, or at least more.

Fog fills the empty spaces between cabins tonight,
and the children walk through it, laughing.
No one runs from shadows in the grey,
nobody gets lost in it and doesn't come back.

But at dawn, looking down to the cabins in the valley,
kid poets squat in the wet grass,
come in late for breakfast, silently.
Who can find fossils anymore?
Who sees the crystals?
We took them all. They are gone.
The places that are empty
wait to be filled.

ERIC SELINGER

The Pictographs in Twin Buttes Canyon

Mountain Utes, Apache, the Wind River Sioux
all followed trails the Anasazi left here.
Today, I work sixty Herefords up this canyon,
watch the white faces of calves dart
through the scrub. Below my right stirrup,
the rhythm of the dog's feet.
I look up to a flash of red
on the sandstone, pictographs
written here two thousand years ago.
I do not know what the language
says, but I might learn something of it
from the bitter smell of sage.
I ride across the tracks of a band
of mustangs, descendants of the tribal stock.
Those tough horses run to keep the words
moving on the land. Above me
a red-tailed hawk whistles. He carries
the tongue in the arch of his shoulders.
He holds nearly nothing and pulls himself
to it, grips the sinking surface of air,
leans his throat across the sky.

                                        ANNE LARSEN

Mute

I read your lips
in the moon's blunt bone.
Shadows shift in your eyes
like gray shades of tempered sterling.
I feel the secrets
of your blue black irises.
Through their gate,
I glimpse the things you've seen without me:
redwoods' deep roots in a river cavern,
the silk tongue of a unicorn,
diamond mines.

You walk away,
like a cream cat,
roaming in dark glasses.

CAROLE HAMNER

An Icelandic Orange

If I gave you an orange,
skin peeled back in angles,
the sections pried slightly,
a handkerchief for dabbing lips dry after tasting,
it would be more real, more fruitful than words.

Think a while:

some Arab children chasing
each other under camels
would join together and surround the orange,
push sandy toes into the skin,
poke at the moist filaments with twenty sticky fingers;
wheat and jam spill over the plate,
seep through the floor and are absorbed in the dust.

And if before I placed your orange in the mail
I wrote: "Iceland" on the envelope,
you would not be able to dream of dusk dances
around oranges. You would see penguins
and fruit. A few whales.

My words could stop your dreams. They have power.
More power than fruit.
Yet, I could not speak to you,
only write my name beside yours,
yet, I could not watch your eyes
as I dot my i's, and I try
to capture the yellow of a yellow bird's wing.

I could not touch your shoulder where it becomes arm,
tell you things about mats or of haddock.
This is not feeling. This is a poem.

I can send you an orange to start your dreams
make them more complicated with cold.
I could send you a letter
make it obscure with line breaks and apples,
a name in a stone jug, contemplations on the limits
of language. Even a few allusions to illusions
of confusion might litter the page.

And all this to say
that I can't find a way
to poetically tell you
I miss you
except
"I miss you."
And I hope this is better than penguins and fruit.

ROD BARR

123

Grassfire

It was
a day that
black smoke swam

in, we
saw it a long
way off, grampa

and me,
and went to
bump across the

roads, in
the forest we
could see the

fire here
and there, a
glance of flame

and grampa
drove quicker, his
Ford had holes

where your
feet go and just
yesterday he hit a

tree, grampa
scares me so much
as he goes down

this road,
all the flames
are open, reaching

for us
from the ditch
on the side and

men in
gray uniforms and
oil spots are talking

to grampa
I'm afraid
the fire is a mile

wide and
calling for me
to wash in it, water

my fears
in its spring,
the fire is so real

I can
see its face through
the men killing it

I'm screaming
and grampa
turns around, turned

back and
he laughs so
long I see

the flame
in his eyes,
burning him out.

DAN WILEY

My Grandmother Fell Out the Parlor Window

I

My grandmother fell
out the parlor window —
She always leaned too far,
like a setter heading into the wind.
I'm sure she used to pray
for the soul of a tree
every Autumn evening. She did love so
to be a squirrel,
    but thought a Hickory tree was better,
for a serious wish,
One day,
she fell out on the azaleas
    and hopped away.

We met again.
Across a crowd, I saw,
She was sitting cross-legged on the carpeting,
telling in a story voice
to a girdled, small-eyed woman.
The woman's lips peeled when
she closed them hard,
as though they were a
Sunday school door
she had wanted to slam.
    I had supposed I was
the only one who saw her
escaping over the flowerbeds
and off into the wild lawn.

JENNIFER VICKERY

The Dead Sheep

In Maine, when the sun had especially
Turned the trees into glass burning upon
My swollen skin, nearly noon, we were walking.

He was talking to me about the sun and
The various ways light reflects off of ice
In the terrifying snow.

It was terrifying. That morning the child
From Maine and the child from New York
With ospreys rubbing their

Breasts against the trees. The salt was
Everywhere, in our eyes. It was then,
When we were circling the rocks in

A small cove at the side of the island
Where the smell of the swamp marsh permeated
The breath of the air, that we approached

An enormous swarm of insects that were feeding
Upon a sheep. Its entrails flowed onto the
Moist sand meeting together under the best

Of circumstances. I was fascinated and repulsed
Noticing a crushed liver where I least expected
It. I nearly wept, believe me, seeing an

Ex-living thing being devoured by a teeming
Explosion of maggots and worms, its sad
Eyes which still had expression

Being tossed about. The sorry mouth caught
On a jagged rock, almost completely white
From the high tide.

The Maine kid looked on with indifference and
Said, "Yes, lots of sheep, they start wandering
And dash their tiny brains on the rocks."

We moved on. We looked out and saw the
Lobstermen in the enormous bay and about
Five miles away the mainland with the spires

And whitened houses like jagged rocks. The
Gray skies almost flooded with ospreys crying
For their young.

CHRIS BOWDY

Hunting After-hours, The Moon Hidden by the Trees

And hasn't the night taken us all
to the side of the road
where a car pulls off onto gravel,
where wheels stir angry green leaves.
The driver lifts a gun from the seat,
makes a second check for his shells.

This man walks into the woods,
his flashlight following fresh deer tracks.
He waits under an oak until a buck
comes to drink from the stream before them.
The man leans forward to press shells into blued
    chambers,
his finger freeing the safety catch:

He remembers his fiancée who calls on weekends,
    whispering
that she will be back when she works things out;
The look on his father's face as he spoke
of leaving the family to look for work;
His friend who went canoeing at night, to be found
the next morning, pulled from heavy water.

The trigger remains still; the air is silent.
This man places his gun on the ground,
turns to walk under shadows,
following his boot tracks to the road.

And when he returns empty-handed,
he will get into his car; he will drive past
other abandoned cars; he will see
that we all walk alone into this silent forest.

CURTIS RIDEOUT

Sakura Matsuri

Sakura Matsuri
Cherry blossoming
if we are too late
the petals become anxious wings
of pink silk that jump from the tree
and fly towards the East
too early
we see winter's bare arms
of the cherry tree
knotted hands, arthritic elbows
brown and rough
and just a hopeful tint of
change and life
and the one more pink Spring
we all were praying for

MELISSA MOSS

I admire the poems in this chapter very much for their compassion, vividness, courage, and humor. These poems make me feel better about people. These poems make my life more interesting. Self-expression benefits the person doing it and, when done well, other people, too. Art is an exchange of our humanness. We need this exchange. Without it, we can all too easily become bored, cynical, and small-minded.

I could tell you many reasons why I admire these poems. But the poems speak very well for themselves. Besides, the poems are already written. I'm interested in the poems that haven't been written — the poems you might write, right now, or maybe months from now. If an idea for a poem starts churning around in your imagination, you may decide that you have to write it down. That's when the fun begins. How will it look on paper? Will you like it? Are you going to be disappointed? Will you be surprised? Is the poem going to be a part of your personal development? I hope this book stimulates you to write down your ideas and feelings. Now, *that* would be a good book. So good luck and good writing.

Index of Poems

At Beth Levin's Farm, Lewisburg, PA
   — John Schulman   83–84

Backyard Dreams — Alleen Barber   34–35
The Bird — Curtis Rideout   16
A Bottle of Memories — Rodney Caulder   89

California Man — James Farrer   77
Cheddar Cheese and Chocolate Cake
   — Juliet Gainsborough   4
Clouds — Helen Gardner   45
Cloudy Fall Days — Amy Albert   20–21
Confusion — Ashley Reaves   104
Counseling at My Old Camp — Eric Selinger   119

A Dancer's World — Tiffani Tennison   39
The Dead Sheep — Chris Bowdy   128–29
Death Wish — Deanne Palas   56
Deer Hunting — Chad Atkins   54
Discovery — Toni Mosley   6–7
Distant Peaches (after a painting by Cézanne)
   — John Schulman   106
Dr. Good Blue — Nancy Watzman   52

Elegy for Grandma — Angela Hoxworth   91–92

Fantasy — Rodney Caulder   69

Fantasy — Elaine Norman   59–60
Father and Daughter — Kyla Boyse   72
Fireflies — Robert Strazds   65–66
Five Finger Exercise — Bonnie Nevel   102

Gonna Bake Me a Rainbow Poem — Amy Wilson   xii
Grandma's Gift — Kate Murdock   87–88
Grassfire — Dan Wiley   124–26
Growing Up — Ashley Reaves   101

Haven's Green — James Farrer   64
Honani — Sibyl Frankenburg   89–91
Hunting After-hours, The Moon Hidden by the Trees
    — Curtis Rideout   130–31

I Am First-Person Singular — Kimberly Roller   8
I Am More Foliage — Edith Lundgreen   101
An Icelandic Orange — Rod Barr   122–23

Jewelry Store — Elizabeth Allen   67–68

Keep Smiling — Julia Browne   73–75

The Last Saturday — Ken Kostka   9
Laughter — Pamela Cobb   18
Let the Geese Fly — Elia Lande   23–24
Like, Am I Noticed — Mike Belanger   30–31
Locked In — Whitney Burry   103

Magenta — Juliet Gainsborough   43
Mute — Carole Hamner   121
My Blind Heart — Charlene Dunlap   42
My Brother's Room — Emily Kolinski   57–58
My Grandmother Fell Out the Parlor Window
    — Jennifer Vickery   126–27
My Hamster Is a Little Like a Bear — Sharon Finley
    78–79
My Undergrad — Jennifer Rudio   76

Night Slavery — Christine McLean   21–23

The Oldest Dancers — Lori Keyes   62–63
On Sunday You'll Be Home — Jenny Connelly   14–15
On the Beach — Juliet Gainsborough   40
Outside the Meat Plant's Walls — Christine
    Murray   98

Photograph (after a line by Laurence Raab)
    — Brian Staker   107
The Pictographs in Twin Buttes Canyon
    — Anne Larsen   120
Poem 2 — Rod Barr   92–93
Prejudice — Kimberly Harmon   41

Reflections in Frost — Lisa Rabin   49–50
Request to a Minstrel — Andrea Cox   27
Reunion — Ken Kostka   99

Sadness — David Awl   44
Sakura Matsuri — Melissa Moss   131
Scene — Mary Beth Carville   20
Seashore Girl — James Farrer   28–29
Sea Sing — Heather Noyes   32
Storms — Margie DeMerell   71
Summer in Kansas — Christine Murray   10
Summer Evening — Kimberly England   85
Sunwashed Windows — Hilwatha Stephens   12
The Surface — Elaine Norman   13–14
Suzy Lynn — Julie Bentley   47–48

Teach Me — Linwood Wells   105
Through Their Eyes — Laurie Flowers   96–97
Tonight the Phone — Lisa Freinkel   82

Untitled *(Sometimes)* — Kyla Boyse   95
Untitled *(These invoices on my insurance)*
    — Lira Tollison   55

135

Untitled *(Walking home from the busstop)*
    — Madelyn Detloff 36–37

Walking in December — Noah de Lissovoy 5–6
What Happens When You Eat Sardines
    — Linwood Wells 60–61
Where Were You Yesterday? — Hilwatha Stephens 81
White — Aliette Scheer 46
Winter Trees — Denise Overfield 117–18

You Haven't Got a Prayer — Margie DeMerell 29–30

Index of Poets

Albert, Amy — *Cloudy Fall Days*   20–21
Allen, Elizabeth — *Jewelry Store*   67–68
Atkins, Chad — *Deer Hunting*   54
Awl, David — *Sadness*   44

Barber, Alleen — *Backyard Dreams*   34–35
Barr, Rod — *An Icelandic Orange*   122–23,
    Poem 2   92–93
Belanger, Mike — *Like, Am I Noticed*   30–31
Bentley, Julie — *Suzy Lynn*   47–48
Bowdy, Chris — *The Dead Sheep*   128–29
Boyse, Kyla — *Father and Daughter*   72,
    Untitled *(Sometimes)*   95
Browne, Julia — *Keep Smiling*   73–75
Burry, Whitney — *Locked In*   103

Carville, Mary Beth — *Scene*   20
Caulder, Rodney — *A Bottle of Memories*   89,
    Fantasy   69
Cobb, Pamela — *Laughter*   18
Connelly, Jenny — *On Sunday You'll be Home*   14–15
Cox, Andrea — *Request to a Minstrel*   27

de Lissovoy, Noah — *Walking in December*   5–6
DeMerell, Margie — *Storms*   71,
    You Haven't Got a Prayer   29–30

Detloff, Madelyn
— Untitled *(Walking home from the busstop)*
36–37
Dunlap, Charlene — *My Blind Heart* 42

England, Kimberly — *Summer Evening* 85

Farrer, James — *California Man* 77,
Haven's Green 64,
Seashore Girl 28–29
Finley, Sharon — *My Hamster Is a Little Like a Bear*
78–79
Flowers, Laurie — *Through Their Eyes* 96–97
Frankenburg, Sibyl — *Honani* 89–91
Freinkel, Lisa — *Tonight the Phone* 82

Gainsborough, Juliet
— *Cheddar Cheese and Chocolate Cake* 4,
Magenta 43,
On the Beach 40
Gardner, Helen — *Clouds* 45

Hamner, Carole — *Mute* 121
Harmon, Kimberly — *Prejudice* 41
Hoxworth, Angela — *Elegy for Grandma* 91–92

Keyes, Lori — *The Oldest Dancers* 62–63
Kolinski, Emily — *My Brother's Room* 57–58
Kostka, Ken — *The Last Saturday* 9,
Reunion 99

Lande, Elia — *Let the Geese Fly* 23–24
Larsen, Anne
— *The Pictographs in Twin Buttes*
Canyon 120
Lundgreen, Edith — *I Am More Foliage* 101

138

McLean, Christine — *Night Slavery*   21–23
Mosley, Toni — *Discovery*   6–7
Moss, Melissa — *Sakura Matsuri*   131
Murdock, Kate — *Grandma's Gift*   87–88
Murray, Christine — *Outside the Meat Plant's
    Walls*   98,
    Summer in Kansas   10

Nevel, Bonnie — *Five Finger Exercise*   102
Norman, Elaine — *Fantasy*   59–60,
    The Surface   13–14
Noyes, Heather — *Sea Sing*   32

Overfield, Denise — *Winter Trees*   117–18

Palas, Deanne — *Death Wish*   56

Rabin, Lisa — *Reflections in Frost*   49–50
Reaves, Ashley — *Confusion*   104,
    Growing Up   101
Rideout, Curtis — *The Bird*   16,
    *Hunting After-hours, The Moon Hidden by the
    Trees*   130–31
Roller, Kimberly — *I Am First-Person Singular*   8
Rudio, Jennifer — *My Undergrad*   76

Scheer, Aliette — *White*   46
Schulman, John
    — *At Beth Levin's Farm, Lewisburg, PA*   83–84,
    Distant Peaches (after a painting by Cézanne)   106
Selinger, Eric — *Counseling at My Old Camp*   119
Staker, Brian
    — *Photograph (after a line by Laurence
    Raab)*   107
Stephens, Hilwatha
    — *Sunwashed Windows*   12, *Where Were You
    Yesterday?*   81

139

Strazds, Robert — *Fireflies* 65–66

Tennison, Tiffani — *A Dancer's World* 39
Tollison, Lira
    — Untitled *(These invoices on my insurance)* 55

Vickery, Jennifer
    — *My Grandmother Fell Out the Parlor Window*
    126–27

Watzman, Nancy — *Dr. Good Blue* 52
Wells, Linwood — *Teach Me* 105,
    What Happens When You Eat Sardines 60–61
Wiley, Dan — *Grassfire* 124–26
Wilson, Amy — *Gonna Bake Me a Rainbow Poem* xii

About the Scholastic Awards Programs

Annually since 1923 Scholastic Inc. has sought to encourage and recognize creative achievement in Writing and Art by students in grades 7–12 in schools across the United States and Canada, and in U.S. schools abroad. More than 400 honors, including cash prizes, gold medal plaques, tuition grants and scholarships, and certificates of merit are awarded each year in the writing awards program.

The writing awards have ten categories. In Group I (for grades 7, 8, and 9) students may enter Essay, Short Story, Poetry, and Dramatic Script. In Group II (for grades 10, 11, and 12) students may enter Short Story, Short-short Story, Poetry, Essay, Humor, and Dramatic Script.

After careful screening of entries by Scholastic editors, the top-ranking manuscripts are sent for final evaluation to panels of nationally known authors, editors, and educators.

Many award-winning entries appear in the pages of Scholastic's magazines, such as *Literary Cavalcade, Scholastic Voice, Scholastic Scope,* and *Junior Scholastic.* A considerable number, like those in this book, are eventually printed in collections and anthologies published by Scholastic.

Students and teachers interested in participating in this program are invited to write for detailed information to: Scholastic Awards Program, 730 Broadway, New York, N.Y. 10003.

Scholastic Inc., the educational publishing company, administers and conducts the yearlong program. Scholastic is the largest publisher of children's classroom magazines and paperback books in the English-speaking world. Scholastic also publishes educational software and video products. The writing awards are co-sponsored by Apple Computer and Smith Corona.

About the Author

Peter Sears is the author of four small books of poetry and, most recently, *Tour: New & Selected Poems* from Breitenbush Books. *Tour* was favorably reviewed by both *Publisher's Weekly* and *Library Journal.* Mr. Sears' poems have appeared in *The Atlantic, Mademoiselle, Saturday Review,* and *Rolling Stone.* He is also the author of *Secret Writing: Keys to the Mysteries of Reading and Writing* from Teachers & Writers Collaborative and has written articles on teaching writing for *Teachers & Writers* magazine. Mr. Sears has served on panels for the National Endowment for the Arts. He has taught English at the middle school and high school levels and creative writing at the college and graduate levels for twenty-five years. His favorite grade level to teach is tenth grade. He was writer in residence at Reed College and director of the writing program at the Chautauqua Writing Institute. He taught in the Language and Thinking Program at Bard College, where he was Dean of Students. Presently, Mr. Sears teaches a course in the teaching of poetry in the MAT Program at Lewis and Clark College and is the Community Services Coordinator at the Oregon Arts Commission. His responsibilities include managing Oregon's Arts-in-Education program. Mr. Sears lives in Portland, Oregon, with his wife, Anita Helle. His daughter, Rivers Sears, is twelve years old.